ADOBE PHOTOSHOP VERSION 2024

Unraveling the Advance Image manipulation of the new version of Adobe Photo shop with AI assistance and other unique creative features

BY:

NELSON TURNE

TABLE OF CONTENT

INTRODUCTION

Adobe Photoshop 2024 stands at the pinnacle of graphic design and image editing software globally, offering an unparalleled suite of features and capabilities. This versatile platform empowers users to engage in a spectrum of creative endeavors with finesse. From the meticulous crafting and enhancement of photos to the intricate development of illustrations and 3D artwork, Photoshop ensures a professional touch in every aspect.

Yet, its prowess extends beyond traditional realms; users can seamlessly venture into the digital frontier by designing captivating websites that reflect their artistic vision. The software's prowess doesn't stop at static imagery; it extends into the dynamic realm of simulated videos, providing a robust toolkit for editing and refining visual narratives.

What truly sets Adobe Photoshop 2024 apart is its transformative ability to turn conceptualization into reality. With a comprehensive set of tools, users can breathe life into their ideas, leveraging the software's advanced features to bring imagination to fruition. In essence, Adobe Photoshop 2024 is not merely a software; it is an artistic enabler, a digital atelier where creativity knows no bounds.

CHAPTER ONE

SYSTEM REQUIREMENT OF ADOBE PHOTOSHOP 2024 FOR macOS

Before installing Adobe Photoshop 2024 Free Download for macOS, it is essential to verify whether your system meets the recommended or minimum system requirements:

- Operating System: macOS Big Sur (version 11.0) or later

- Memory (RAM): 8 GB of RAM required.

- Hard Disk Space: 8 GB of free space required.

- Processor: Multicore Intel® or Apple Silicon processor (2 GHz or faster processor with SSE 4.2 or later) with 64-bit support.

- Screen Resolution: A display of 1024 x 768 pixels (1280×800 recommended) with 16-bit color support.

- Additionally, the system should be OpenGL 2.0-capable.

INSTALLING AND LAUNCHING ADOBE PHOTOSHOP 2024

To successfully install and effectively make use of Adobe Photoshop 24, the following are the steps you should follow

1. Sets the stage for a seamless process by advising the user to initiate the disabling of Gatekeeper, ensuring a hurdle-free installation experience.
2. Implement the installation of AntiCC v5.9, a powerful tool designed for optimal performance and backed up for security on OneDrive. This step emphasizes the importance of incorporating

reliable backup mechanisms into your process, providing an added layer of assurance.

3. A pivotal moment in your installation endeavor that allows you to execute the installation file with precision by right-clicking and selecting the 'Open' option. This deliberate action ensures a meticulous initiation, setting the stage for a successful integration of AntiCC v5.9 into your system. Embrace the process with confidence, knowing that each step is a deliberate move towards a fortified and functional system.

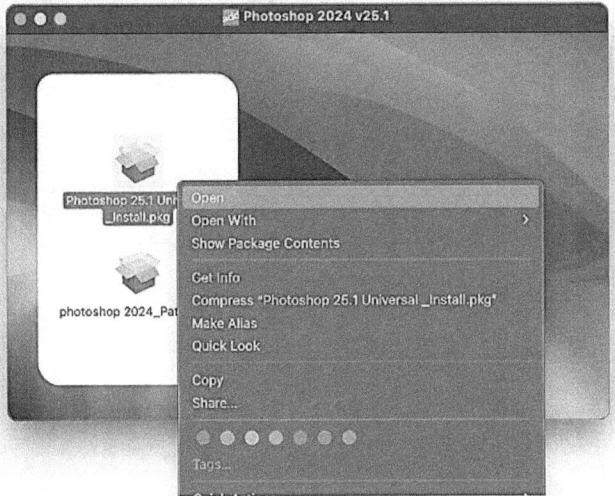

4. Following installation, refrain from running the P4tch; instead, launch Photoshop. A login screen resembling the following will promptly present itself

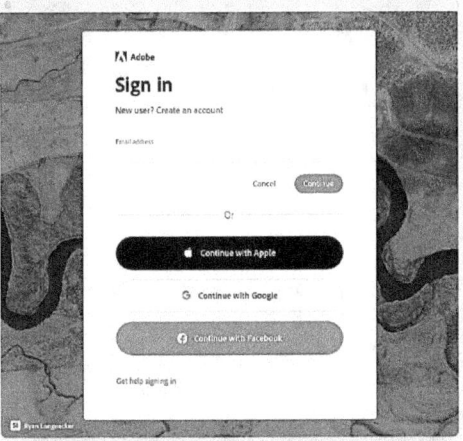

- Opt for the "Login with Google" option (or choose Apple, Facebook, or your preferred platform). Don't fret about using an expired account – the system accommodates it seamlessly. Upon successful login, the interface will transition to the informative "Let's get you..." screen, guiding you through essential setup steps. Once this phase is complete, feel free to elegantly conclude the process by closing the application. This ensures a comprehensive and user-friendly experience in setting up your account within the application.

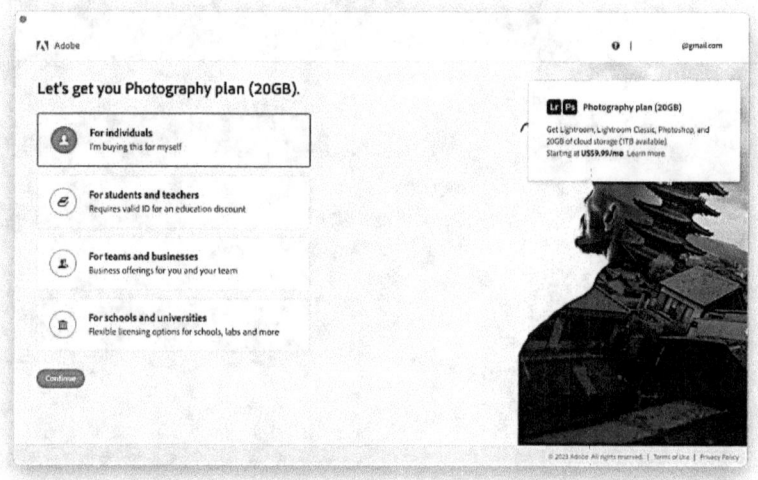

ACTIVATING ADOBE 2024

Ensure that steps one and two of the above are properly followed and the proceed in running the install command, press y and then enter >enter the password and wait for the installation to finish.

```
=========================
= Adobe Script Installer =
========= 1.1 ===========

Detected Architecture: arm64
Hash Verification: Passed

Start installation now?[Y/n]:y

[Password:
Installation starts...
Exit Code: 0

Installation complete successfully!

Saving session...
...copying shared history...
...saving history...truncating history files...
...completed.
```

- Run the P4tch

Execute the P4tch file to complete the process. Take care not to impact other software installations by paying attention to these two specific locations during the installation.

FEATURES OF ADOBE PHOTOSHOP 2024

GENERATIVE AI

Turn your wildest dreams into stunning images effortlessly with Generative Fill – an extraordinary generative AI tool. This feature supercharges your creativity and streamlines your workflow by employing straightforward text prompts for intricate edits, yielding high-quality results. Modify, expand, or eliminate content in images nondestructively, ensuring you retain ultimate control. Explore the versatility of Generative Fill both locally and online through Photoshop on the web. And also, this remarkable tool elevates your creative journey.

Generative Fill represents a cutting-edge feature within Photoshop, harnessing the power of advanced generative algorithms. This functionality enables users to seamlessly and automatically generate content within the software, marking a significant leap in the evolution of creative tools. The essence of Generative Fill lies in its ability to intelligently analyze and understand the context of an image, allowing it to produce new elements or fill specific areas with generated content.

Key Aspects of Generative Fill

1. **Automated Content Generation:** Generative Fill operates as a sophisticated automation tool, sparing users the intricacies of manual content creation. Through intricate algorithms, it examines the existing elements within an image, comprehends their spatial relationships, and intelligently generates additional content to enhance or complete the visual composition.

2. **Contextual Understanding:** One of the standout features is its contextual understanding. The algorithm doesn't merely produce content randomly; instead, it interprets the context of the image. This means it considers factors such as color schemes, textures, and patterns, ensuring that the generated elements seamlessly integrate with the existing visual narrative.

3. **Versatility in Application:** The application of Generative Fill spans a spectrum of creative endeavors. Whether users aim to fill in gaps in an image, expand upon existing elements, or experiment with entirely new design elements, the versatility of this tool positions it as an indispensable asset for both novice and expert users.

4. **Enhancing Creative Workflows:** By automating certain aspects of content generation, Generative Fill significantly enhances creative workflows. Designers and artists can expedite their processes, experiment with novel ideas, and achieve results that might have been time-prohibitive through traditional manual methods.

5. **Iterative Design Exploration:** Furthermore, Generative Fill encourages iterative design exploration. Users can iterate through various generative outputs, fine-tuning their creative vision with each iteration. This iterative approach fosters a dynamic and experimental creative process, allowing users to discover unforeseen possibilities.

In essence, Generative Fill redefines the creative landscape within Photoshop, providing users with a powerful and intelligent tool to augment their artistic endeavors. Its nuanced understanding of context and automated content generation capabilities contribute to a more efficient, explorative, and imaginative design process.

Another standout feature in this 2024 edition is the "match color" functionality, empowering users to effortlessly adjust image colors using pre-set options or customize them with a single click.

- Match color" functionality, empowering users to effortlessly adjust image colors using pre-set options or customize them with a single click.

GENERATIVE CREDIT IN PHOTOSHOP

Adobe is introducing Generative credits, a concept similar to a phone or data plan. Think of it like having an unlimited data plan that provides unrestricted data usage. However, once you surpass a certain threshold, the speed may be moderated during peak times.

For paid subscribers, fast processing credits will be available. Beyond this limit, you can continue generating without incurring extra costs, but the processing speed may decrease if server demand is high.

Notably, these credits are free of charge, and your allotment will refresh or "top off" each month. It's important to note that credit accumulation and rollovers are not permitted.

The specific monthly credit allocations are outlined in the chart available on Adobe's website, and additional information can be found in the FAQ section.

This new system will take effect on November 1, 2024. Key allocations include:

- Full Creative Cloud (CC): 1000 Credits per month.
- Single app (e.g., Photoshop): 500 Credits per month.

- Photography + Lightroom CC: 250 Credits per month. New subscribers after November 1 will receive 100 Credits per **month.**

Plan	Monthly generative credits
Creative Cloud All Apps	1,000
Creative Cloud Single App • Illustrator, InDesign, Photoshop, Premiere Pro, After Effects, Audition, Animate, Adobe Dreamweaver, Adobe Stock, Photography 1TB	500

Creative Cloud Single App
• Creative Cloud Photography 20GB:
  • Subscribers before November 1, 2023
  • Subscribers after November 1, 2023
	250
	100

Creative Cloud Single App • Lightroom	100

What Happens If You Deplete Your Credit Balance

To be frank, most individuals won't exhaust 1000 or even 250 credits per month. But suppose you do reach that limit—what happens next? You can continue utilizing the feature, but be prepared for potential slowdowns or even a daily cap (although the specifics of this cap are unknown since it hasn't been implemented yet; my assumption is that it aims to prevent system abuse, such as establishing a generation farm for selling as stock).

In the event of significant speed throttling, there's an alternative— you can purchase additional credits for $4.99 per month, providing you with 100 more credits. Essentially, this grants you priority processing, allowing you to move to the front of the line when utilizing your monthly credits. These credits refresh monthly, akin to the minutes on a phone plan.

It's important to note that Generative credits specifically apply to Generative Fill and Generative Expand, excluding the Remove tool and other AI features in Photoshop. In Adobe Express and Firefly, they also extend to Text effects and Text-to-image.

To utilize Generative Fill, start by creating a selection around the object or area in your image using one of Photoshop's selection tools. Once you've made your selection, you can proceed in one of the following ways:

Start by using any of Photoshop's selection tools to outline the specific object or area within your image that you want to work on. This selection acts as the target for Generative Fill.

Once your selection is in place, you can access Generative Fill through various methods, including.

- **Contextual Task Bar**: Click on the Generative Fill button in the contextual task bar that appears when you've made the selection. This button typically provides quick access to the tool.
- **Application Bar:** Alternatively, you can go to the "Edit" menu in the application bar and select "Generative Fill." This option is available in the main menu for more comprehensive control.
- Right-Click Menu: If you prefer, you can right-click within the selection while holding the Ctrl key (or Right+click on your mouse) and choose "Generative Fill" from the context menu. This provides a convenient way to access the tool using a contextual menu.

Once you've chosen your preferred method to access Generative Fill, you can proceed to make adjustments, add, extend, or remove content within the selected area using simple text prompts, all while retaining the original image non-destructively. This feature is designed to be intuitive and user-friendly, making complex image editing tasks more accessible to a broader range of users.

TOOLS, OPTIONS, AND CONTEXTUAL TASKBAR

Remove People or Objects From Photos With Generative Fill

Generative Fill is a remarkable, creativity-driven tool that empowers you to non-destructively add, extend, or remove content from your images. It operates through straightforward text prompts, generating astonishingly realistic results that are bound to amaze and delight you, all in a matter of seconds.

Here's a guide on employing Photoshop's Generative Fill to eliminate individuals or objects from your photo. While the emphasis here is on removing people, the steps remain consistent regardless of what element you aim to remove.

Let's begin with this image sourced from Adobe Stock. It's the same image featured in my Content-Aware Fill tutorial, but this time, we'll utilize Generative Fill to erase two of the three people from the picture.

- Opt for the Lasso Tool To commence, create a selection outline around the person or object slated for removal. Navigate to the toolbar and select the Lasso Tool. If you've utilized Photoshop's Select Subject command or the Object Selection Tool, an additional step is necessary for optimal results. I'll illustrate the reason behind this and elucidate the extra step shortly.

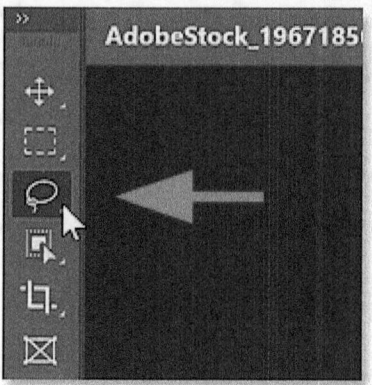

- Outline the Person or Object Subsequently, draw a selection outline around the targeted person or object. In my case, I'll be selecting the woman on the right. Ensure that the selection encompasses some of the surrounding areas. Generative Fill relies on this additional space to discern the AI-generated content's appearance and seamlessly blend it with the surrounding environment.

Observe as I intentionally include part of the background in my selection.

Here's the completed selection, which also encompasses the shadow under her left foot. It's essential to include the shadow, as removing the person without the corresponding shadow would appear unnatural.

- Access Generative Fill in the Contextual Task Bar Locate Photoshop's Generative Fill feature in the recently introduced Contextual Task Bar, positioned directly below your selection outline.

If the Contextual Task Bar isn't visible, navigate to the Window menu in the Menu Bar and ensure that "Contextual Task Bar" is checked.

Next, within the Task Bar, select the Generative Fill button.

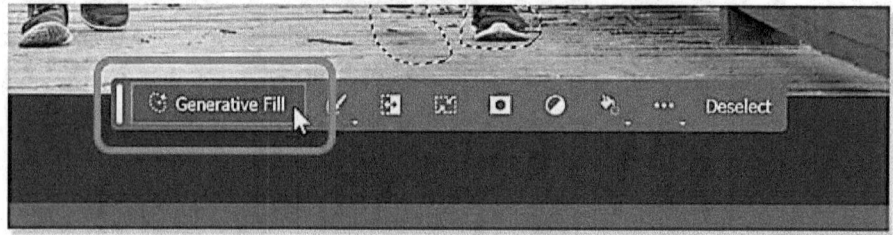

- Activate the Generate Button A prompt box emerges, allowing you to provide a description of what you want Generative Fill to introduce to the selected area. However, when removing a person or object, leave the prompt box empty, indicating to Photoshop to fill the region with new content harmonizing with the surrounding elements.

Subsequently, click the Generate button.

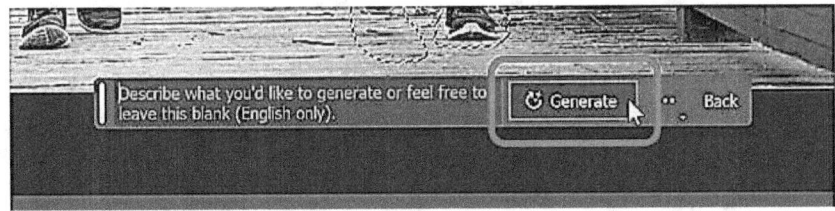

Photoshop transmits the image to Adobe's servers via the internet, where new AI-generated content is crafted. A progress bar appears, typically taking 10-15 seconds, contingent on your internet speed.

Once the progress bar vanishes, the person or object is seamlessly erased from the photo, replaced with meticulously generated AI content. The result often appears so seamless that it erases any trace of their presence.

In my example, Photoshop filled the void with new grass, added plants in the background, and incorporated intricate details into the bridge where the woman was originally walking. Notably, the new content even aligns with the depth of field of the original photo, maintaining a pleasing background blur.

Contextual Taskbar

In the latest update, Photoshop introduces a feature that adds a layer of personalization and convenience to your workspace—the ability to pin the Contextual Menu to a specific area, offering a tailored and consistent layout for your creative endeavors. What sets this enhancement apart is its lasting impact; even after closing and reopening the program, Photoshop retains the carefully chosen placement of your Contextual Menu.

The process is simple yet transformative. Begin by dragging the menu to your preferred location within the workspace, aligning it precisely where you find it most ergonomic or visually accessible. Once satisfied with the placement, click on the three dots situated on the right of the menu. From the ensuing options, select "Pin bar position." This action secures the menu in its current spot, ensuring it remains fixed until you decide otherwise.

This newfound ability to pin the Contextual Menu not only allows for a more personalized and intuitive workspace but also introduces a level of consistency that streamlines your creative process. Whether you're meticulously retouching images, fine-tuning compositions, or exploring advanced features, having the menu steadfastly positioned at your preferred location enhances efficiency and fosters a more seamless workflow.

To revert to the default arrangement or explore new placements, simply follow the same straightforward steps, unchecking the "Pin bar position" option. This dynamic feature empowers you to adapt your workspace to your unique preferences, providing an additional layer of control over the Photoshop environment. It's a subtle yet impactful improvement that contributes to an enhanced user experience and a more tailored approach to your creative projects.

NEW DOCUMENT WORKFLOW

Open image/file workflow

Here's a step-by-step elaboration on how to open an image file in Adobe Photoshop, after launching Adobe Photoshop on your computer:

File Menu: In the top menu bar of Photoshop, locate and click on "File." This action will open a dropdown menu with various file-related options.

From the "File" dropdown menu, choose **Open**. You can do this by either clicking on "Open" directly using your mouse or by using the keyboard shortcuts: "**Ctrl+O**" on Windows or "Command+O" on a Mac.

This action prompts a standard file dialog box to appear on your screen.

Navigate to Your File: In the file dialog box, you need to navigate to the folder where the image file you want to open is located. This involves browsing through your computer's file directory structure.

Select the Image File: Once you're in the appropriate folder, look for the specific image file you wish to open.

- Click on the file's name to select it. The selected file will be highlighted.

Open Button: To confirm your selection and open the chosen image file in Photoshop, locate and click the "Open" button within the file dialog box.

Type tool workflow

The impact of AI on the workflow of photographers and graphic designers

Adobe Sensei AI powers several recent additions, including a one-click background or sky selection tool. Additionally, there's a selection of new Artistic Effect options, all driven by AI. Adobe's goal with these is to let users effortlessly enhance their images by adding effects inspired by renowned works of art or popular art styles with just a simple click.

OPENING PHOTOSHOPS

Files can be accessed in Photoshop through the Open command or the Open Recent command. Additionally, integration with other Adobe applications such as Illustrator, Fresco, Lightroom, or Bridge allows for seamless file opening.

For specific file types like camera raw and PDF, users can customize settings and options in a dialog box before the files fully load in Photoshop.

Beyond still images, Photoshop extends its capabilities to video files and image sequence files, providing users with the flexibility to open and edit a variety of visual content.

Occasionally, Photoshop might struggle to identify the accurate format for a file, especially if it has been transferred between different operating systems, such as from Mac OS to Windows. In instances where the file format is mislabeled due to such transfers, it becomes necessary to manually specify the correct format before opening the file.

Most importantly you should not that Photoshop relies on plug-in modules to open and import various file formats. If a particular file format is not visible in the Open dialog box or the File > Import submenu, it could indicate the need to install the corresponding plug-in module for that format.

You have the option to preserve (when applicable) layers, masks, transparency, compound shapes, slices, image maps, and editable type when transferring your Illustrator artwork to Photoshop. To achieve this, export your artwork from Illustrator in the Photoshop (PSD) file format. However, in cases where your Illustrator art includes elements not supported by Photoshop, the visual appearance of the artwork will be maintained, but the layers will be combined, and the artwork will be rasterized.

Here's a step-by-step guide on how to open a file in Adobe Photoshop:

- Launch Photoshop: Open Adobe Photoshop on your computer.
- Access the "File" Menu: In the top menu bar, locate and click on "File." This will reveal a dropdown menu.
- Select "Open": From the "File" menu, choose "Open." Alternatively, you can use the keyboard shortcuts: "Ctrl+O" on Windows or "Command+O" on a Mac.
- Navigate to Your File: A standard file dialog box will appear. Browse to the folder where your desired file is stored.

- Select the File: Click on the name of the file you want to open. This will highlight your selection.
- Click "Open": To confirm your choice and open the selected file in Photoshop, find and click the "Open" button within the file dialog box.

Now, the chosen file will be loaded into Adobe Photoshop, and you can start working on it based on your editing or design requirements.

Open a file with the use of the Open command

- Go to File > Open.
- Pick the file you wish to open. If it's not visible, choose the option to display all files from the Files Of Type (Windows) or Enable (Mac OS) pop-up menu.
- Click Open. In certain instances, a dialog box may appear, allowing you to configure format-specific options.

Open a Recently Used File

Navigate to File > Open Recent and choose a file from the displayed submenu.

If you wish to control the number of files listed in the Open Recent menu, modify the Recent File List Contains option in the File Handling preferences. Access this by selecting Edit > Preferences > File Handling on Windows, or Photoshop > Preferences > File Handling on Mac OS.

Make A Specification Of The File Format In Which The File Should Be Opened

If a file was saved with an extension incongruent with its actual format (e.g., a PSD file with a .gif extension) or lacks an extension altogether, Photoshop might encounter difficulty opening it. To ensure successful recognition and opening, it's crucial to select the correct format that corresponds to the file.

Follow one of the methods below:

In case a file has been saved with an extension that doesn't accurately represent its true format (e.g., a PSD file saved with a .gif extension) or lacks an extension altogether, Photoshop might encounter difficulty opening the file. Ensuring the correct format is selected will enable Photoshop to accurately identify and open the file.

Follow one of the procedures below

- Navigate to File > Open As.
- Choose the file you wish to open.
- From the Open As pop-up menu, select the desired format.
- Click Open to proceed.

For Mac OS:

- Go to File > Open.
- Select All Documents from the Show pop-up menu.
- Pick the file you intend to open.
- From the Format pop-up menu, choose the correct file format.
- Click Open to initiate the opening process.

If you encounter difficulty opening the file, it could be due to a discrepancy between the chosen format and the actual format of the file, or the file may be damaged. It's essential to ensure that the selected format accurately reflects the file's true format. Additionally, file damage could hinder the opening process, and in such cases, you might need to explore file recovery or repair options to address any potential issues.

OPEN PDF FILE

The Adobe Portable Document Format (PDF) is a versatile file format capable of representing both vector and bitmap data, equipped with electronic document search and navigation features. It stands as the primary format for Adobe Illustrator and Adobe Acrobat.

PDF files exhibit variability, ranging from single-image documents to those with multiple pages and images. When opening a PDF file in Photoshop, you have the flexibility to select specific pages or images and define rasterization preferences.

Moreover, PDF data can be imported using the Place command, Paste command, or drag-and-drop functionality. The imported page or image is placed on a distinct layer as a Smart Object.

Please note: The subsequent procedure is specifically for opening generic PDF files in Photoshop. For Photoshop PDF files, no specific options need to be specified in the Import PDF dialog box.

The following procedures can be of help

For Photoshop

- Navigate to File > Open.
- In the Open dialog box, choose the desired file, and click Open.

For Bridge

- In Adobe Bridge, pick the PDF file.
- Select File > Open With > Adobe Photoshop.

Skip to step 3.

In the Import PDF dialog box:

Under Select, opt for either Pages or Images, depending on the specific elements you wish to import from the PDF document.

Click on the thumbnails to choose the pages or images for opening. Use Shift-click to select multiple pages or images. The count of selected items is displayed under the preview window.

You can utilize the Thumbnail Size menu to modify the thumbnail view within the preview window. Opting for the Fit Page option accommodates one thumbnail within the preview window, and a scroll bar becomes visible if there are multiple items.

Proceed to step 8 if you are importing images.

Adjust the thumbnail view in the preview window by using the Thumbnail Size menu. Selecting the Fit Page option places one thumbnail in the preview window, and a scroll bar appears for multiple items.

Name the new document by entering text in the Name text box. If importing multiple pages or images, several documents will open with the base name followed by a number. In the Page Options section, use the Crop To menu to define the included part of the PDF document:

Bounding Box: Crops to the smallest rectangular region containing all text and graphics, eliminating white space and elements outside the Trim Box.

Please be aware that the Bounding Box option won't crop white space integrated into a background generated by the source application.

- Media Box: Crops to the original size of the page.
- Crop Box: Crops to the clipping region (crop margins) of the PDF file.
- Bleed Box: Crops to the region specified in the PDF file to account for production process limitations like cutting, folding, and trimming.

- Trim Box: Crops to the region specified for the intended finished size of the page.
- Art Box: Crops to the region specified in the PDF file for placing the PDF data into another application.

In the Image Size section, input values for Width and Height as needed:

- To maintain the aspect ratio of pages while scaling within the defined rectangle, choose Constrain Proportions.
- If you want to scale pages precisely to the Width and Height values without maintaining the aspect ratio, unselect Constrain Proportions. Note that some distortion may occur during scaling.

When multiple pages are chosen, the Width and Height text boxes show the maximum values. If Constrain Proportions is selected and the Width and Height values remain unchanged, all pages will be rendered at their original size. Modifying the values will proportionately scale all pages during rasterization.

Define the following options in the Image Size section:

Resolution: Determines the resolution for the new document. Refer to information about pixel dimensions and printed image resolution.

Mode: Establishes the color mode for the new document. Explore details on color modes.

Bit Depth: Specifies the bit depth for the new document. Learn more about bit depth.

The final pixel dimensions of the resulting document are determined by the Width and Height values along with the specified Resolution.

To prevent color profile warnings from appearing, choose the "Suppress Warning" option. After making this selection, proceed by clicking the "OK" button to confirm and apply the changes.

OPEN AN EPS FILE

EPS, short for Encapsulated PostScript, serves as a versatile format capable of representing both vector and bitmap data. Widely supported across graphic, illustration, and page-layout programs, Adobe Illustrator is a notable application for producing PostScript artwork. Upon opening an EPS file containing vector art, a rasterization process occurs, transforming the mathematically defined lines and curves into the pixels or bits constituting a bitmap image.

Incorporating PostScript artwork into Photoshop is facilitated through various methods such as the Place command, Paste command, and drag-and-drop functionality.

Here's a step-by-step guide:

- Navigate to File > Open in Photoshop.
- Select the specific file you wish to open and click the "Open" button.
- Specify the desired dimensions, resolution, and color mode. To maintain the original height-to-width ratio, opt for "Constrain Proportions."
- To reduce the appearance of jagged lines at the edges of the artwork, enhance the rendering quality by selecting the "Anti-aliased" option. This helps to create smoother transitions between contrasting pixels.

HOW TO SAVE YOUR WORK

Efficiently manage and preserve alterations in your Photoshop documents by employing the diverse Save commands tailored to your preferred format or future accessibility requirements.

When saving a file in Photoshop, explore the options within the File menu and select from the range of Save commands available, including Save, Save As, or Save a Copy. Once you've chosen a save command, the flexibility extends to deciding whether to Save to Creative Cloud, ensuring seamless cloud-based access, or Save on your computer for localized storage and convenience. This versatility empowers you to tailor your saving process based on your specific workflow and storage preferences.

Save

To securely preserve modifications made to your document while maintaining its existing format, follow these steps: Navigate to the File menu and opt for the "Save" command. This action ensures that your changes are seamlessly stored within the current file format, offering a straightforward and efficient method to update your document without altering its original structure.

Save as

When desiring to save a file under a distinct name, location, or format, follow these comprehensive steps:
1. Select File > Save As from the menu.

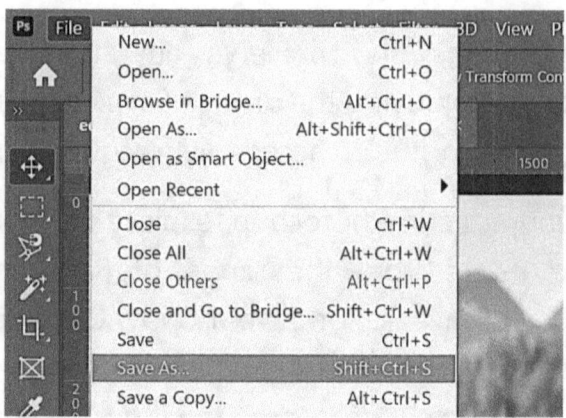

2. From the Format menu, pick the desired file format that aligns with your requirements.

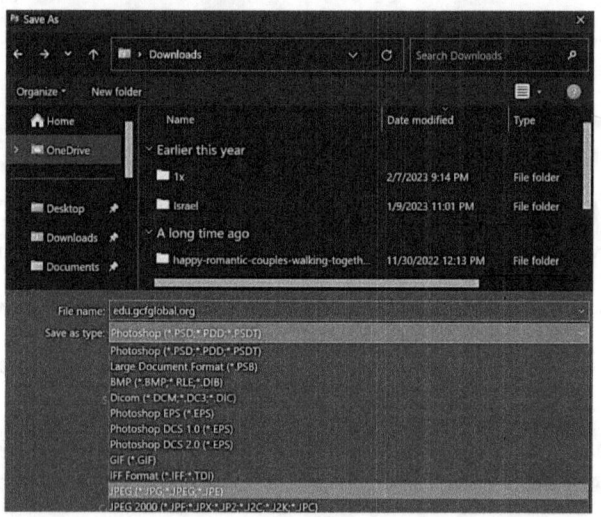

3. Specify a distinctive filename and designate the preferred location for the saved file.
4. Within the Save As dialog box, fine-tune your saving options according to your preferences.

5. Conclude the process by clicking the Save button. In certain image formats, a dialog box may appear, providing additional options to customize your saving preferences further.

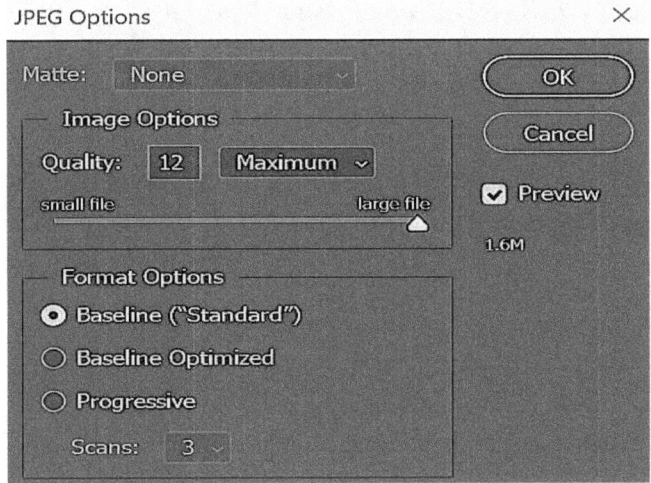

This thorough approach ensures a tailored and precise saving procedure for your file.

Adobe Photoshop (*.psd) Files

Unlocking a seamless integration between Adobe® Photoshop® (.psd) files and SOLIDWORKS, you can both import Photoshop files and save various SOLIDWORKS data, encompassing sketches, parts, assemblies, and drawings, in the Adobe Photoshop format. Furthermore, SOLIDWORKS data stored as Adobe Portable Document Format (.pdf) files seamlessly interfaces with Photoshop.

Here's an in-depth guide to utilizing these functionalities:

Importing Photoshop Files

- Go to File > Open to initiate the import of Photoshop files into SOLIDWORKS.

- For 3DEXPERIENCE Users: If the Open from 3DEXPERIENCE dialog box surfaces, select This PC.
- Specify Files of type as Adobe Photoshop Files (*.psd).

Saving SOLIDWORKS Data as Photoshop Files

- Click File > Save As to preserve SOLIDWORKS data in the Photoshop format.
- For 3DEXPERIENCE Users: If the Save As New dialog box appears, choose Save to This PC.
- For Save as type, opt for Adobe Photoshop Files (*.psd).
- Click Options to delve into TIFF, Photoshop, and JPEG Export Options.

Handling Multi-Layer Photoshop Files

- Single-layer and multi-layer Photoshop images are seamlessly imported as SOLIDWORKS Sketch Pictures.
- For multi-layer Photoshop files, you have the flexibility to handpick specific layers for import, and these layers seamlessly amalgamate into a unified image within SOLIDWORKS.

Utilizing Photoshop Files in SOLIDWORKS

- Leverage the versatility of Photoshop files as image backgrounds within SOLIDWORKS.
- Navigate through the Decals menu for incorporating Photoshop file types into images and masks.
- Explore the Materials menu, where Photoshop file types are readily available for integration.

This comprehensive approach ensures not only a fluid interchange between Photoshop and SOLIDWORKS but also empowers you with a myriad of options for handling and enhancing your design workflow.

Save a Copy

If you wish to transform a layered file into a flat file, it's necessary to generate a new version of the document. In case the desired format, such as JPEG or PNG, is not visible, employ the "Save a Copy" option for all formats. This facilitates the creation of a preserved version of your document. To execute this, follow these steps:

1. Navigate to File > Save a Copy.
2. Alternatively, you can utilize the Save a Copy button located under the Save As dialog box.

FILE SAVING PROPERTIES

Unlock a multitude of file-saving possibilities through the Save As and Save a Copy dialog boxes in Photoshop. The availability of these options is contingent upon both the specific file being saved and the chosen file format.

Key Options Include

Alpha Channels:

- Saves alpha channel information along with the image.
- Impact when Disabled: Disabling this option removes alpha channels from the saved image.

Layers

Preserves all layers within the image.

- If this option is disabled or unavailable, visible layers undergo flattening or merging (based on the selected format).

Notes: Ensures the retention of notes along with the image.

Spot Colors

Saves spot channel information embedded in the image.

Disabling this option results in the removal of spot colors from the saved image.

These customizable options empower users to tailor the saving process according to their specific needs, providing a nuanced approach to handling diverse file formats and compositions in Photoshop.

File Saving Preferences

File preference topically depends on your operating system:

- For Windows, navigate to Edit > Preferences > File; While
- For macOS, Head to Photoshop > Preferences > File Handling.

Choose from the following options for saving image previews:

- Never Save and preserve files without including previews.
- Always Save, save files with specified previews.
- Ask When Saving, Opt for assigning previews on a file-by-file basis. In Mac OS, you have the flexibility to select one or more preview types.

File Extension (Windows)

Select from the following options for the three-character file extensions denoting a file's format:

Use Upper Case: Append file extensions using uppercase characters.

Use Lower Case: Append file extensions using lowercase characters.

Append File Extension (Mac OS)

File extensions are crucial for files intended for use on or transfer to a Windows system. Choose one of the following options for appending extensions to filenames:

- Never: Save files without file extensions.
- Always: Append file extensions to filenames.
- Ask When Saving: Append file extensions on a file-by-file basis.

Additionally, opt for Use Lower Case to append file extensions using lowercase characters.

Save to Original Folder

By default, when saving, Photoshop directs to the folder where images originated. If you wish to default to the folder you last saved in, unselect this option.

Save in Background

Enable background saving to continue working in Photoshop seamlessly after initiating a Save command. This eliminates the need to wait for Photoshop to complete the saving process.

Automatically Save Recovery Information

Photoshop offers automatic storage of crash-recovery information at specified intervals. In the event of a crash, this ensures that your work is recovered when you restart Photoshop. Adjust the interval based on your preferences for optimal file recovery.

SAVING LARGE DOCUMENTS

In the realm of document creation, Photoshop provides robust support for documents containing images up to a staggering 300,000 pixels in either dimension. This expansive capability is particularly advantageous for projects requiring high-resolution and intricate details.

For images surpassing the 30,000-pixel threshold in either dimension, Photoshop extends its versatility by offering three distinct file formats tailored to accommodate these substantial dimensions. It's important to note, however, that the seamless handling of such sizable files is a unique strength of Photoshop and may not be universally supported across various applications. Commonly, other software applications, and even earlier versions of Photoshop predating Photoshop CS, grapple with limitations, particularly concerning files larger than 2 GB or images exceeding the 30,000-pixel mark in either dimension. Therefore, while Photoshop excels in handling these expansive dimensions, compatibility considerations become crucial when collaborating or sharing files across different platforms and software versions.

When opting for a file-saving strategy in Photoshop, navigate to File > Save As, and explore the following formats to tailor your document preservation:

Large Document Format (PSB):

PSB supports documents of virtually any file size, offering unparalleled flexibility for expansive projects.

All Photoshop features are meticulously preserved within PSB files. However, it's worth noting that certain plug-in filters may be inaccessible if the documents exceed 30,000 pixels in width or height.

Presently, PSB files are exclusively supported by Photoshop CS and subsequent versions, emphasizing the need for an updated environment to leverage this format's capabilities fully.

Photoshop Raw

Photoshop Raw accommodates documents with any pixel dimension or file size, showcasing its adaptability to a wide range of creative endeavors.

With regards to Layer Consideration, While Photoshop Raw supports expansive dimensions, it doesn't preserve layers in the saved files. Large documents saved in this format are automatically flattened for simplicity.

TIFF (Tagged Image File Format)

Size Limit: TIFF supports files up to an impressive 4 GB in size, making it suitable for substantial projects.

Limitation: It's important to note that TIFF has a size constraint, and documents larger than 4 GB cannot be saved in this format. Therefore, for extremely large projects, alternative formats like PSB may be more suitable.

Note: Every file format available in Photoshop presents unique advantages and considerations. The selection of the most suitable format hinges on the particular demands of your project, requiring thoughtful consideration of elements such as file size, feature preservation, layer considerations, and compatibility across various versions of Photoshop.

EXPORT LAYERS TO FILES

Numerous situations may necessitate exporting your layers to individual files in Photoshop. The conventional method of exporting merges layers into a single document. To achieve the export of each layer as an individual file, you must employ an alternative export process.

- Navigate to File > Export > Layers To Files. If you have your project with multiple layers, simply access File > Export > Layers to Files from the top bar.

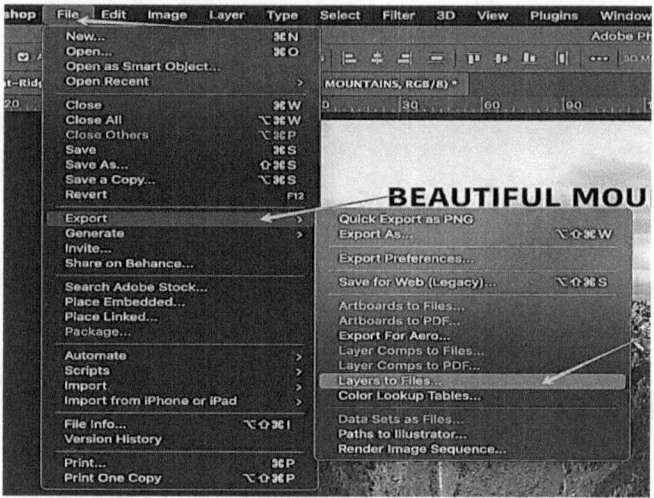

- Choose a File Format. A dialog box will appear, offering various export options for you to select.

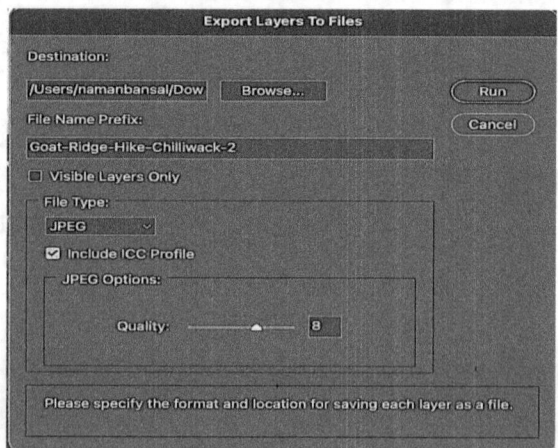

Begin by choosing the desired file format for layer export through the "File Type" option in the export window. Given Photoshop's extensive range of file formats, here's a breakdown of some popular ones:

- Now that you've picked a file type, designate the location for saving your exported layers. Click the 'Browse' button to navigate and select a location on your computer.

CLARIFICATION ADOBE CAMERA RAW

Adobe Camera Raw serves as a sophisticated plugin seamlessly integrated into the Adobe Photoshop environment, providing users with a powerful platform to execute nuanced and impactful edits on their photographic compositions. One of its pivotal features lies in the non-destructive nature of the edits, affording users the convenience of effortlessly reverting changes without any impact on the original files.

In essence, envision Adobe Camera Raw as a highly adept image processor that takes the raw data captured by the camera and transforms it into a malleable and editable image. This processed image then becomes the canvas on which Photoshop can perform a myriad of manipulations.

This versatile tool finds application in a broad spectrum of tasks, showcasing its capabilities in tasks such as precise cropping, meticulous sharpening, establishing optimal white balance, fine-tuning contrast levels, executing intricate color adjustments, and navigating through tonal range alterations. Beyond these fundamental functions, Adobe Camera Raw is a robust ally in a plethora of other photo enhancement processes, contributing to a comprehensive and dynamic editing experience for photographers and digital artists alike.

What are Raw Images

Raw" images serve as the digital counterparts to traditional film negatives, offering a level of artistic flexibility and control unparalleled in comparison to JPG files. While JPG files typically lack the same degree of creative freedom, tools like Camera Raw become essential for professional photographers seeking to shape and refine their images according to their artistic vision.

Raw files represent the unprocessed and uncompressed digital images generated by a camera, preserving the unaltered data captured by the camera's image sensor. Distinguished by their larger file size in comparison to JPEG files, raw files offer a wealth of advantages due to their comprehensive retention of the original image data.

The intrinsic value of raw files becomes apparent in their ability to retain intricate image details that might be lost in a JPEG file. Unlike JPEG, raw files preserve the complete range of data captured by the camera, providing a robust foundation for post-processing and editing. This remarkable feature allows photographers and digital artists to uncover and recover subtle nuances, tones, and details that might otherwise remain unseen in a more compressed and processed format like JPEG.

In essence, the capacity to extract "unseen" information from raw files transcends the limitations of conventional file formats, offering a reservoir of untapped potential for creative exploration and refinement in the realm of digital imagery. This characteristic makes raw files an indispensable asset for those seeking to maximize the depth and quality of their photographic work during the post-production phase.

As an illustration, consider a photograph where the initial appearance presents an overexposed scene with a blown-out sky, as observed in the image on the left side. Through a straightforward adjustment of sliders within the Camera Raw interface, I successfully restored a previously obscured and exquisite blue sky adorned with fluffy clouds.

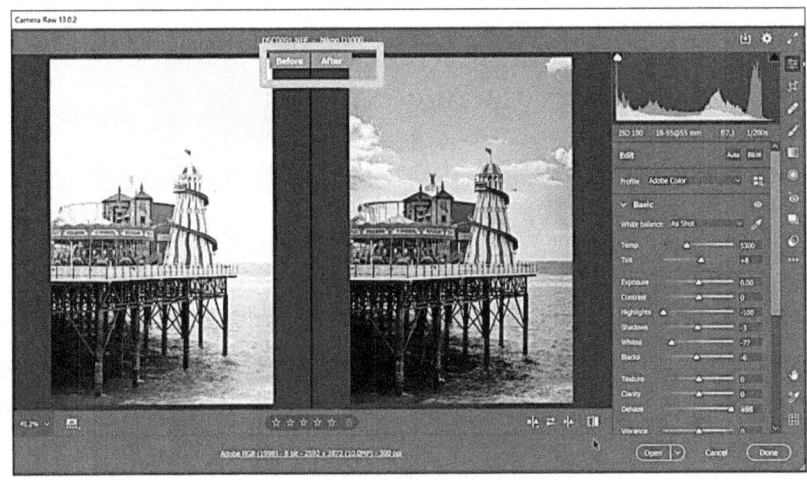

Why should Camera Raw be used to edit pictures

Camera Raw provides a swift and efficient platform for editing and enhancing raw files sourced from digital cameras. Additionally, the Adobe Camera Raw filter enables the editing of JPEG and TIFF files within the Photoshop environment.

A key advantage of utilizing Camera Raw for photo editing, as opposed to direct editing in Photoshop, lies in its non-destructive editing approach. This means that the original photograph remains unaltered and undamaged throughout the editing process. Furthermore, Camera Raw offers editing features not present in Photoshop, enhancing its versatility.

During the editing process in Camera Raw, adjustments are saved as a set of instructions applied to the photo, allowing users to witness a live preview of the changes as they work. The beauty of non-destructive editing becomes evident as users can revisit and modify their edits endlessly, or even reset changes entirely, all without causing any harm to the original pixels. This flexibility and preservation of the original image make Camera Raw a highly valuable tool in the realm of digital photography and post-processing.

Importantly, If you have prior experience with Adobe "Lightroom", you'll find Camera Raw to be highly familiar, as they essentially function as the same entity. Both applications share identical image-processing technology, with Adobe Lightroom being constructed using the same raw image-processing technology found in Adobe Camera Raw.

How to Use CUBE LUTs in Adobe Camera Raw

Now, let's explore the process of importing CUBE files into Camera Raw. While these files are commonly used in video editing, using them in Camera Raw involves an additional step of conversion. Follow these steps:

1. Open Photoshop and either create a new project or open an existing image. The image type doesn't matter; it's just needed as a placeholder.

2. Navigate to "Filter" and select "Camera Raw Filter." This action opens the image in Camera Raw.

3. In the Camera Raw interface, click on "Profiles" from the sidebar. To create a new profile, hold down the ALT key while clicking on the "Create Preset" button.

4. In the popup window, go to the bottom and check the box for "Color Lookup Table." Subsequently, your file explorer will appear, allowing you to load a CUBE file. Provide a name for the profile; for instance, "Sunset," matching the LUT's name. Choose or create a folder for organization; in this example, "Colorful LUTs Pack" is used for a set like the Filtergrade LUTs pack.

5. Return to the main editing screen, and you can now select a profile as before. Click on "Browse," and open the new folder you created to access the imported filters.

It's worth noting that this method takes longer compared to simply dragging all your LUTs into a folder. The process needs to be repeated for each CUBE file, but once done, the editing interface remains consistent.

LAUNCHING PHOTOSHOP'S CAMERA RAW FORMAT

Opening Images

To process raw images using Camera Raw, begin by selecting one or more camera raw files in Adobe Bridge. Then, choose File > Open In Camera Raw or use the shortcut Ctrl+R (Windows) or Command+R (Mac OS). Once you've made adjustments in the Camera Raw dialog box, click Done to confirm changes and close the dialog. Alternatively, you can click Open Image to open a modified copy of the image in Photoshop.

For processing JPEG or TIFF images in Camera Raw, select the desired files in Adobe Bridge and follow the same steps mentioned above. After adjustments, click Done to accept changes and close the dialog box. You can set preferences for automatically opening JPEG or TIFF images with Camera Raw settings in the JPEG and TIFF Handling section of the Camera Raw preferences.

Importing Camera Raw Images into Photoshop:

To import camera raw images into Photoshop, select the files in Adobe Bridge, and choose File > Open With > Adobe Photoshop CS5. Alternatively, you can use the File > Open command in Photoshop and browse to select camera raw files. After adjustments in the Camera Raw dialog box, click Open Image to apply changes and open the adjusted image in Photoshop. Press Alt (Windows) or Option (Mac OS) to open a copy without saving adjustments to the original image's metadata. Shift-click Open Image to open the image as a Smart Object in Photoshop. Double-click the Smart Object layer to adjust Camera Raw settings at any time.

Additional Tips:

- To open a camera raw image in Photoshop from Adobe Bridge without the Camera Raw dialog box, shift-double-click the thumbnail.

- Hold down Shift while choosing File > Open to open multiple selected images in Photoshop.

Importing Camera Raw Images into After Effects:

For After Effects, select one or more camera raw files in Adobe Bridge and choose File > Open With > Adobe After Effects CS5. Alternatively, use the File > Import command in After Effects and browse to select camera raw files. After adjustments in the Camera Raw dialog box, click OK to confirm changes.

Importing TIFF and JPEG files into After Effects using Camera Raw involves choosing the File > Import command, selecting All Files, choosing Camera Raw from the Format menu, and clicking Open.

To import Camera Raw images into After Effects as a sequence, choose File > Import, select the images, choose Camera Raw Sequence, and click Open. The Camera Raw settings from the first file apply to the entire sequence, except when an XMP sidecar file is present for subsequent frames, in which case, the specific frame uses the settings from the XMP or DNG file.

Save a Camera Raw Image in Another Format

Saving a Camera Raw Image in Another Format:

To convert and save camera raw files from the Camera Raw dialog box, you have the option to choose from PSD, TIFF, JPEG, or DNG formats.

When utilizing the Save Image command in the Camera Raw dialog box, files are queued for processing and saving. This proves beneficial when working on multiple files in the Camera Raw dialog box and saving them in a consistent format.

Follow these steps in the Camera Raw dialog box:

1. Click the Save Image button located in the lower-left corner.

Note: Alt-click (Windows) or Option-click (Mac OS) Save to bypass the Camera Raw Save Options dialog box during the saving process.

2. In the Save Options dialog box, specify the following options:

- Indicates where to save the file. Use the Select Folder button to navigate to the desired location.

- Defines the filename using a convention including elements like date and camera serial number, promoting organized file management.
- Select the desired file format from the Format menu.
- Saves a copy of the camera raw file in the DNG file format.

Compatibility

Specifies the versions of Camera Raw and Lightroom that can read the file. If Custom is chosen, indicate compatibility with DNG 1.1 or DNG 1.3. The default conversion uses lossless compression, preserving information while reducing file size. Opting for Linear (Demosaiced) stores the image data in an interpolated format, enabling compatibility with other software even without a specific camera profile.

JPEG Preview

Embeds a JPEG preview in the DNG file. If chosen, you can specify the preview size. This allows other applications to view the contents of the DNG file without parsing the camera's raw data.

JPEG Saving Format

This option saves duplicates of the camera raw files in the JPEG (Joint Photographic Experts Group) format. To determine the compression level, input a value between 0 to 12 or select from the menu. Opting for a higher value, High, or Maximum results in reduced compression, increasing file size, and maintaining higher image quality. The JPEG format is widely used for showcasing photographs and continuous-tone images in web galleries, slide shows, presentations, and various online services.

TIFF Format

This choice saves duplicates of the camera raw files in the TIFF (Tagged-Image File Format) format. Specify whether to employ no compression or choose LZW or ZIP file compression. TIFF is a versatile bitmap image format supported by nearly all paint, image-editing, and page-layout applications. It offers superior compression and compatibility with other applications compared to the PSD format.

Photoshop Format

This selection saves duplicates of the camera raw files in the PSD file format. You can indicate whether to retain cropped pixel data within the PSD file.

3. After making your selections, click Save.

CHAPTER TWO

WHAT TO KNOW ABOUT PIXEL ART

Pixel art goes beyond being a mere composition of pixels; it's an artistic form that captures the essence of early computer and video game visuals. This encompasses the entire spectrum from classics like Pong to iconic characters such as Sonic the Hedgehog.

In the early days of video games, constrained by lower resolutions, artists faced the challenge of revealing the inherent limitations of pixelated graphics in creations like Space Invaders and Donkey Kong. Pixel art emerged as a creative solution born out of necessity. The artists of the 1970s and 1980s had to pioneer innovative techniques, distilling images to their core elements. A handful of red pixels could convey Mario's distinctive hat, while just a pixel or two would signify his hands or face.

During the 16-bit era of the 1990s, pixel art transformed, becoming more intricate while retaining its essence. Artists now had a larger canvas to explore, yet the fundamental approach persisted: meticulously working with individual pixels, each contributing significantly to the crafting of the overall image.

START DRAWING WITH PIXELS

Creating pixel art demands a meticulous level of precision. Unlike a painter who can employ broad strokes, a pixel artist must meticulously consider the placement of each individual pixel in their composition. A proficient pixel artist can capture the essential form of a subject while skillfully simplifying it.

Embark on your pixel art journey by studying the pixelated characters that have inspired you from the works of past artists. According to pixel artist Emi Monserrate, "References from real life don't apply as nicely in pixel art as they do in other digital art disciplines. You have to learn ways of simplifying complex shapes such as hands or facial expressions."

While recreating classic pixel art can be a meticulous process, following the pixelated path of another artist can be enlightening. It's crucial, however, to refrain from presenting copied work as your own. When working with existing art, it is essential to appropriately credit the original creators.

MAKING PIXEL ART IN PHOTOSHOP

Crafting pixel art in Photoshop becomes straightforward once you establish a canvas tailored for pixelated images.

1. Begin by opening a new canvas.

2. Set up a grid, opting for pixels instead of inches.

3. Adjust subdivisions to one.

4. Modify the image interpolation setting to Nearest Neighbor (preserve hard edges).

5. Utilize the Pencil tool to maintain crisp edges. This leverages its ability to preserve hard edges and provide detailed control over individual pixels.

These steps create a canvas with a grid of individual pixels, providing a foundation for designing retro images. With these settings, you can steer clear of unintended blurring and blending effects.

INTRODUCTION TO PHOTOSHOP'S PENCIL TOOL

In the expansive toolkit of Adobe Photoshop, the Pencil tool stands out as an indispensable instrument for digital artists and designers. This versatile tool offers a unique combination of precision and creative control, allowing users to craft intricate designs, fine details, and pixel-perfect artwork with ease.

The Adobe Photoshop Pencil tool is not merely a virtual drawing implement; it's a gateway to a world of artistic expression. Whether you're aiming for precise line work, intricate shading, or detailed pixel art, the Pencil tool provides the means to bring your vision to life on the digital canvas.

In this exploration, we delve into the capabilities of the Adobe Photoshop Pencil, uncovering its features, functionalities, and the myriad ways it empowers artists to achieve unparalleled precision in their digital creations. Whether you're a seasoned professional or an aspiring artist, the Adobe Photoshop Pencil tool beckons as a versatile and essential companion in the realm of digital artistry.

Steps to use the pencil tool

- **Duplicate the Layer** Begin by duplicating the layer using Ctrl/Cmd+J.

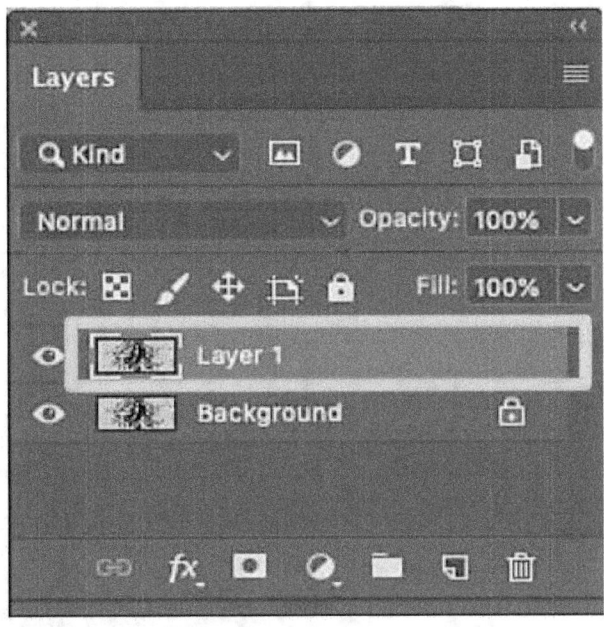

- **Convert to Black and White** Convert the new layer to black and white with Ctl/Cmd+Shift+U.
- **Duplicate Black and White Layer** Duplicate the black and white layer with Ctrl/Cmd+J, resulting in two black and white layers.

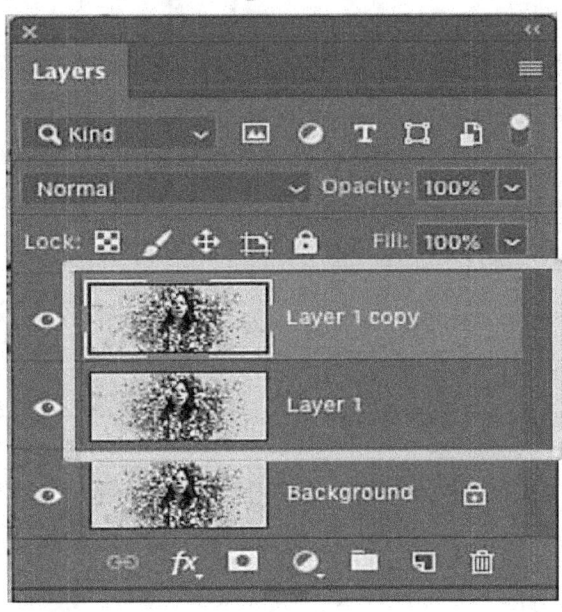

- **Invert the Top Layer** Invert the top black and white layer using Ctrl/Cmd+I.

- **Change Blending Mode to Color Dodge** Change the blending mode to Color Dodge by clicking on Normal in the Layers panel.

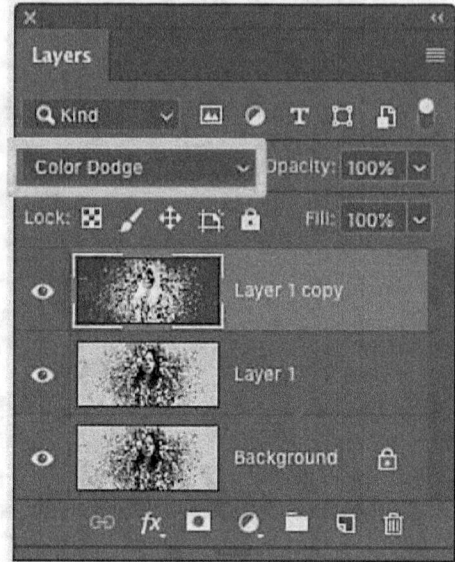

- **Apply Gaussian Blur** Go to Filter > Blur > Gaussian Blur and adjust the slider for a thin, clear outline.

- **Adding the Shading** Group in both black and white layers (Ctrl/Cmd+G) for an organization.

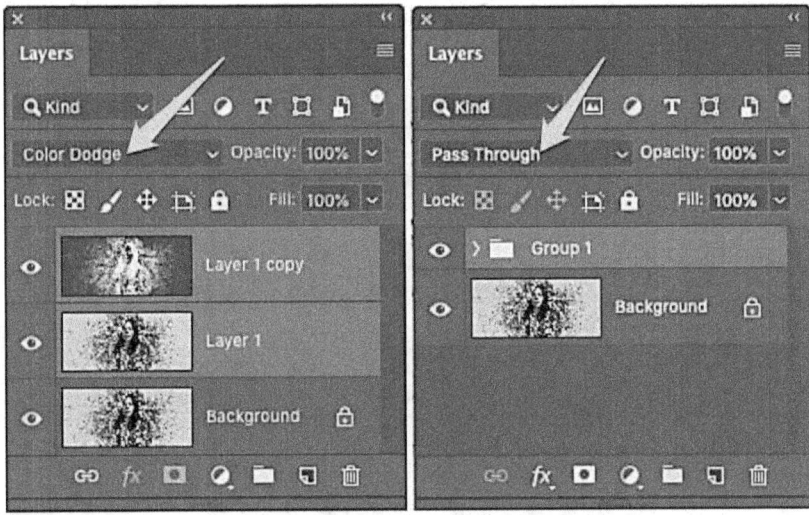

- **Duplicate the Group** Duplicate the group with Ctrl/Cmd+J.
- **Blur the Top Layer in the Group** Choose the top layer in the duplicated group and apply Gaussian Blur for gentle shading.
- **Blend the Two Layer Groups** Select the top group and change the blending mode to Darken. Adjust opacity for a perfect match.
- **Duplicate the Top Layer Group** Duplicate the top layer blending mode for a third group with Ctrl/Cmd+J.
- **Blur the Top Layer in the New Group** Choose the top layer in the new group and apply Gaussian Blur for the final shading.
- **Masking the Effect** Add a layer mask to the top layer group. Hold Alt/Option and click the new layer mask icon for an inverted mask.
- **Painting Shading with Mask** With a soft-edged brush, set the foreground color to white, and opacity to 30%, and paint on the images to add shading.

Adding Edge Sharpening a/ Select all layers and press Ctrl+Alt+Shift+E (Windows) or Cmd+Option+Shift+E (Mac) to create a new composite layer.

b/ Change the layer blending mode to Overlay.

c/ Choose Filter > Other > High Pass.

d/ Adjust the amount for a sharp edge effect.

DRAW CURVES WITH THE PENCIL TOOL

Draw straight lines followed by curves

- **Activate the Pen Tool (P)** Commence by opening your project or creating a new document, then navigate to the Pen Tool (P) located in the Toolbar.

- **Change the Mode to Shape** In the Options Bar, the Mode is initially set to Path. Click the drop-down arrow and switch the mode to Shape. The Options Bar will adjust to display the Shape settings.

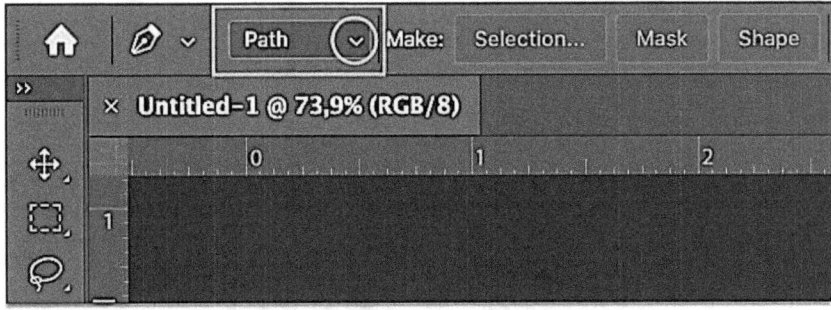

The Options Bar will adjust to display the Shape settings.

- **Set the Shape Fill to Transparent** Now, set the shape's Fill to Transparent. Click the Fill box in the Options Bar, opening a panel with various shape fill options. Choose the Transparent icon, the first from the left.

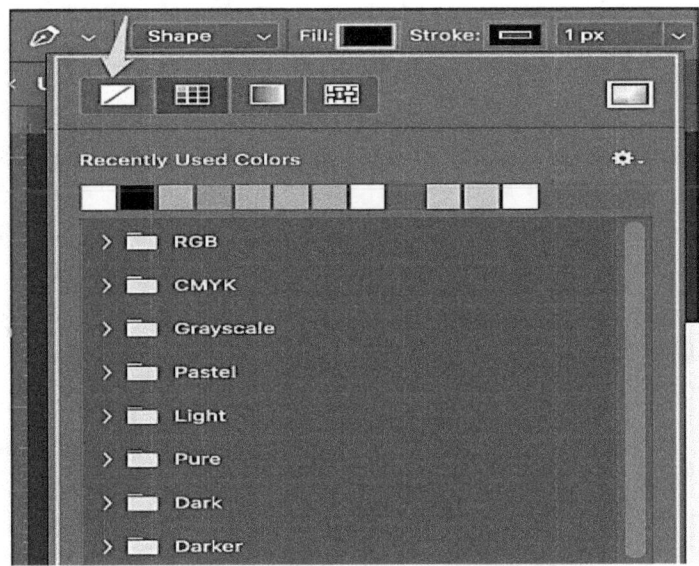

- **Set the Stroke to a Solid Color** Adjust the appearance of your line by configuring the stroke settings. In the Options Bar, change the stroke's Color by clicking the Stroke Fill Box and selecting from the options. Define the line's thickness in pixels by entering a number or dragging the toggle along the width slider. You can revisit and modify the line's appearance after drawing it on your document.

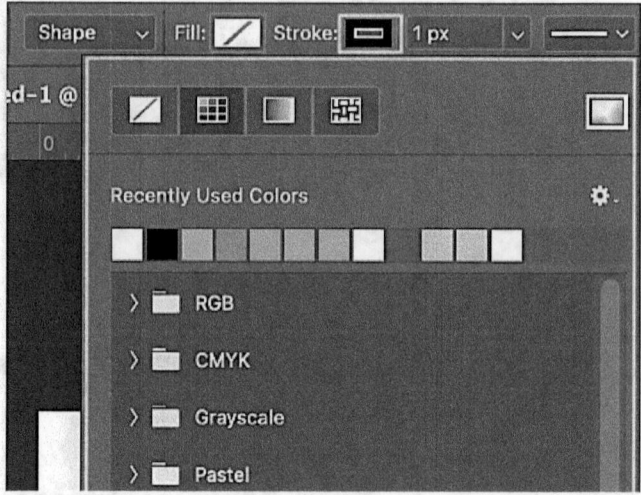

- **Add an Anchor Point** Click on your canvas to add an anchor point, establishing the starting point of your line.

- **Add a Second Anchor Point** Click on another area of your canvas and drag up or down to curve your pen path, creating a curved line since a stroke fill is applied to your pen path. Add more anchor points if desired, clicking and dragging to continue the curve.

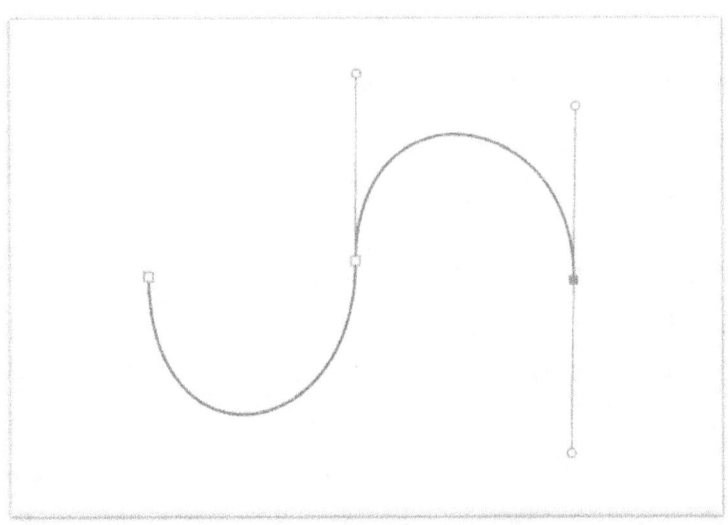

- **Change the Line's Appearance within the Stroke Settings (Optional)** After creating the line, head to the Options Bar to further adjust the stroke settings. For example, modify the color and thickness by changing the stroke fill and adjusting the thickness within the stroke width setting box. This allows you to alter the line's appearance while maintaining the same path.

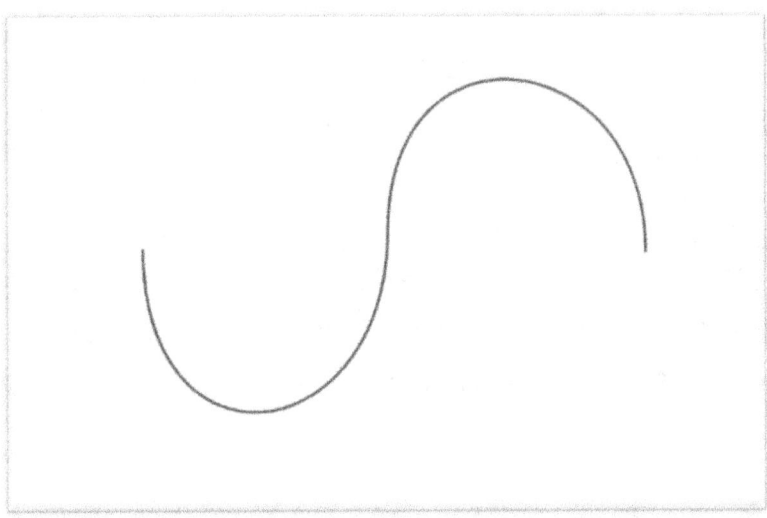

HOW TO CHANGE IMAGE RESOLUTION USING ADOBE PHOTOSHOP

Resolution for printing

After selecting the desired resolution for your print, adjusting your image in Photoshop becomes a straightforward process. With your document open in Photoshop, navigate to the Image menu and select Image Size. Alternatively, you can use the keyboard shortcut Command + Option + I (or Ctrl + Alt + I for PC users).

This action will prompt Photoshop to open the Image Size dialog window, displaying various information about your image, such as pixel dimensions, current resolution, and print size.

An important next step is to uncheck the box labeled Resample. This step is crucial because, when modifying the pixel density of the image, you want to avoid inadvertently altering its pixel dimensions at the same time.

Once you've unchecked the Resample box, the dialog window will refresh, indicating that the Width, Height, and Resolution fields are presently interconnected.

Adjust the Resolution field to align with your preferred resolution, such as 300 pixels per inch in this instance. As you input the new Resolution value, the Width, and Height values will automatically adjust to reflect the updated print size of your document.

CHAPTER THREE

HOW TO RESAMPLE AN IMAGE SIZE

MAKING CHANGES TO THE PIXEL DIMENSIONS OF AN IMAGE

Resizing images is a task that can be approached with relative ease, particularly when utilizing software applications such as Photoshop. However, delving into the intricacies of resizing is essential to maintain the quality of your images.

Within the Photoshop interface, the image resizing feature is strategically positioned in the primary navigational menu, accessible through the path "Image > Image Size." Upon activating this command, a dialog window unfolds, revealing crucial details like the pixel dimensions of your document or image, along with its corresponding file size. This comprehensive view empowers users to make informed decisions when adjusting the dimensions, ensuring that the visual integrity of the image is preserved throughout the resizing process.

Pixel Dimensions

As evident, my image's file size is 72.8 megabytes, with dimensions of 4368 x 2912 pixels. Clicking on "pixels" offers a percentage-based resizing option, though I've personally found it less practical.

When resizing images for the web, attention to pixel dimensions becomes crucial, aligning with monitor and screen resolutions.

For an optimal approach, utilize Photoshop's "Save for Web" command found in the main menu under "File." Yet, if your images prove excessively large, consider preemptively adjusting the resolution with the "Image Size" option before employing the "Save for Web" function.

Altering the pixel dimensions of an image not only impacts its onscreen size but also influences both its image quality and printed characteristics, including printed dimensions or image resolution.

- Navigate to Image > Image Size.
- To preserve the current aspect ratio of pixel width to pixel height, activate Constrain Proportions. This ensures automatic adjustment of the width as the height is modified.
- In the Pixel Dimensions section, input values for Width and Height. If you prefer to input values as percentages of the current dimensions, select Percent as the unit of measurement. The new file size for the image will be displayed at the top of the Image Size dialog box, with the old file size in parentheses.
- Ensure that the Resample Image is enabled and select an interpolation method.
- If your image includes layers with applied styles, choose Scale Styles to proportionally adjust the effects in the resized image. Note that this option is available only when Constrain Proportions is selected.
- Then press OK

Change the Print Dimensions and Resolution

When preparing an image for print media, it's advantageous to define the image size based on the printed dimensions and image resolution, collectively known as the document size. These measurements dictate the overall pixel count and consequently influence the file size of the image.

The document size also establishes the foundational dimensions when placing an image into another application. While you can adjust the scale of the printed image through the Print command, any modifications made using this command solely impact the printed image and not the document size of the image file.

Enabling resampling provides the flexibility to independently alter print dimensions and resolution, effectively changing the total pixel count in the image. Conversely, disabling resampling allows you to adjust either the dimensions or the resolution, with Photoshop automatically adapting the other value to maintain the total pixel count.

For optimal print quality, it is advisable to initially modify the dimensions and resolution without resampling. Resampling should be applied only as needed to achieve the desired result.

Top Tips on Changing Image Resolution

When preparing an image for print media, it is advantageous to define the image size in terms of both the printed dimensions and the image resolution. These combined measurements, collectively referred to as the document size, play a pivotal role in determining the overall pixel count and consequently influence the file size of the image.

The document size not only serves as a foundation for the total pixel count but also establishes the baseline at which the image is integrated into another application. While you can further adjust the scale of the printed image using the Print command, it's essential to note that any modifications made through this command solely impact the printed image and do not alter the document size of the image file.

Enabling resampling for the image provides the flexibility to independently adjust print dimensions and resolution, thereby altering the total pixel count in the image. On the other hand, disabling resampling allows you to modify either the dimensions or the resolution, with Photoshop automatically adjusting the other value to maintain the overall pixel count.

For optimal print quality, it is recommended to initially adjust the dimensions and resolution without resampling. Resampling should only be applied as necessary to preserve the highest quality in the final printed output.

- Navigate to Image > Image Size.

- Modify the print dimensions, image resolution, or both:
   a. To adjust only the print dimensions or resolution while proportionally altering the total pixel count, enable Resample Image and select an interpolation method.
   b. To modify the print dimensions and resolution without changing the total pixel count, disable the Resample Image.
- To preserve the current aspect ratio of the image width to height, activate Constrain Proportions. This ensures that the width adjusts automatically as the height is changed.

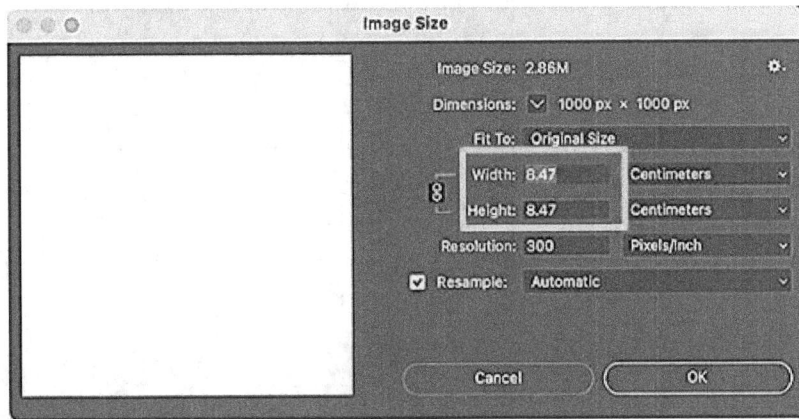

- In the Document Size section, input new values for the height and width. Optionally, select a different unit of measurement. If altering the Width, the Columns option uses the specified width and gutter sizes from the Units & Rulers preferences.
- Specify a new value for Resolution, and if needed, choose a different unit of measurement.

HOW CAN A PICTURE BE RESIZED IN PHOTOSHOP WITHOUT INFLUENCING ITS QUALITY

One approach to achieve this is by utilizing software such as Photoshop, where you can resize an image without compromising its quality through the "Image Size" dialog box.

a. To access the "Image Size" dialog box in Photoshop, open an image, navigate to the "Image" menu dropdown, and then select "Image Size"

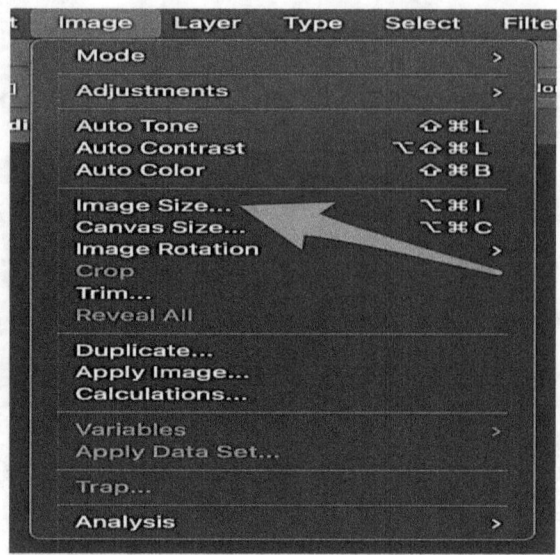

b. Within the "Image Size" dialog box, you have the flexibility to adjust the image's width, height, and resolution, with the resolution representing the number of pixels per inch. A higher resolution implies more pixels, contributing to enhanced image quality.

Firstly, ensure that the "Resample Image" checkbox remains unchecked

c. This checkbox signifies Photoshop's intent to alter the pixel count. When left unchecked, Photoshop retains the original pixel count, preserving image quality and file size.

d. Proceed by selecting a unit of measurement for resizing the image. Click the dropdown next to either "Width" or "Height" to reveal the available options. By default, "Inches" is selected, reflecting Photoshop's focus on print media. Note that with the "Resample" checkbox unchecked, you cannot choose pixels as the unit of measurement

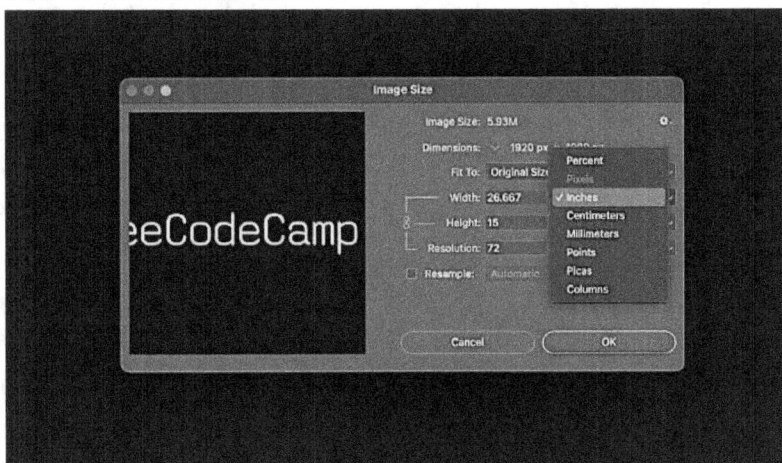

e. Upon selecting a unit of measurement, adjust either the width or height and the other dimension will automatically update.

f. Finally, click the "OK" button to execute the image resizing

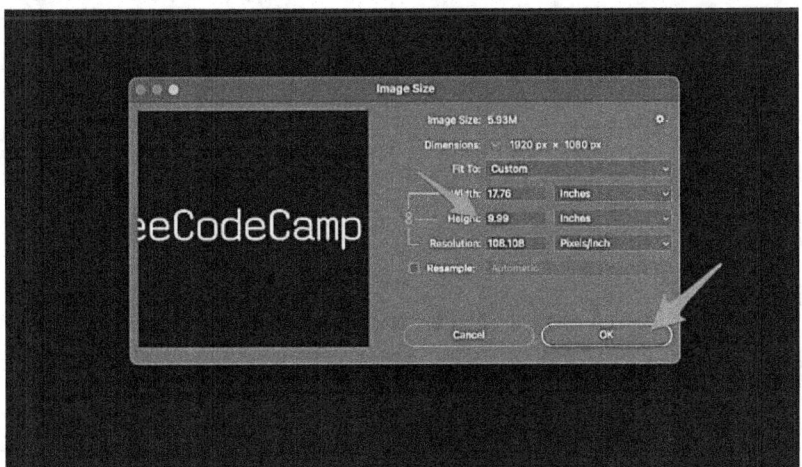

However, in situations where a slight reduction in quality is acceptable, such as when resizing an image for a website, you may opt to check

the "Resample" checkbox. Then, choose pixels as the unit of measurement and proceed with resizing as outlined above

TRANSFORM TOOLS

Adobe Photoshop stands out as a premier raster image editing software meticulously crafted by Adobe Systems. As a quintessential component of Adobe's suite, Photoshop is the go-to choice for graphics editing professionals. Renowned for its robust capabilities in raster graphics editing, Photoshop offers a plethora of exciting features that significantly facilitate the creative process during various projects.

Among its arsenal of tools, the Transform tools stand out as indispensable assets, elevating the user experience and streamlining workflow within the software. These tools empower users to navigate seamlessly through their projects, providing a suite of functions that enhance precision, flexibility, and efficiency in the editing process. Through these transformative features, Adobe Photoshop emerges as a dynamic platform, fostering creativity and enabling professionals to achieve remarkable results in their graphic editing endeavors.

RESIZING A PICTURE USING WITH THE USE OF THE TRANSFORM TOOL

- Positioned at the pinnacle of the working interface is the Menu bar, a comprehensive ribbon housing various menus tailored for managing diverse parameters within the software workflow.

Directly beneath this, we encounter the property bar associated with the active tool, serving as a dynamic platform for effecting changes in the parameters specific to the currently engaged tool. Further down, the layout unfolds into three distinct sections. On the left, the tool panel unfolds, presenting an array of tools designed for diverse editing tasks within the software. In the center, the display window takes precedence, providing a real-time visual representation of the ongoing work. Completing this arrangement, the right side accommodates additional panels, including the color panel and layer panel, alongside others, each contributing to the overall efficiency of our work. It is worth noting that the flexibility of this interface allows users to customize the arrangement of these sections according to their specific preferences and project requirements, providing a tailored and user-centric experience.

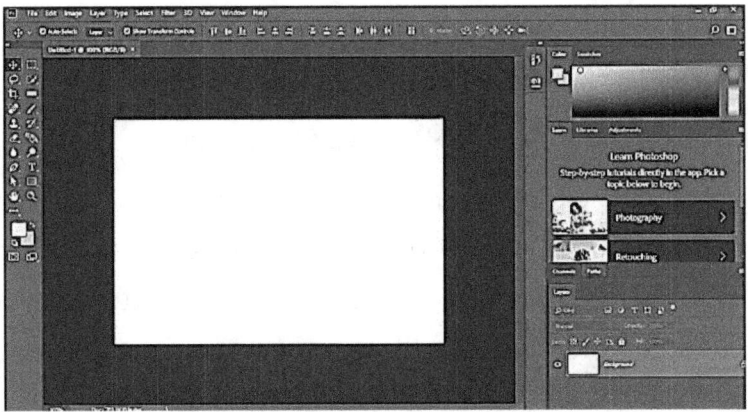

- Moving forward, let's introduce an image into the software to facilitate our learning process. To accomplish this, navigate to the folder where you have stored the image. Once there, utilize the left button of your mouse to select your preferred image. With the image selected, seamlessly transport it into the software's display window area by releasing the mouse button, effectively dropping the image into the interface for further manipulation and exploration.

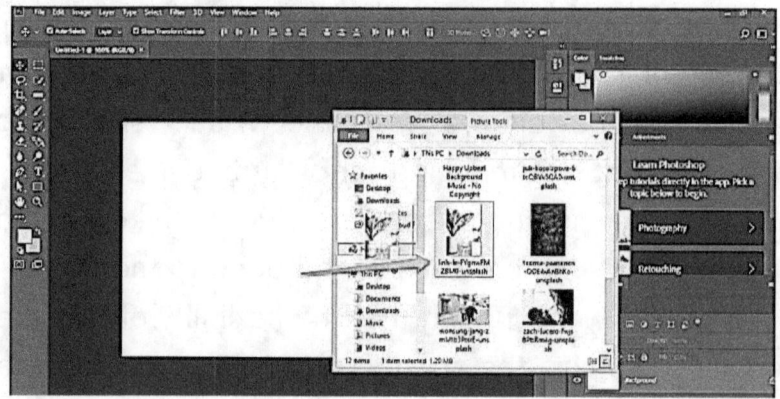

- After depositing the image into the display window area, the image will appear within a bounding box adorned with transformative anchor points, as illustrated. By relocating the anchor point of this bounding box, you gain the ability to scale the image either up or down.

Should you wish to preserve the aspect ratio of the image—maintaining the proportional relationship between width and height—simply press and hold the shift button on your keyboard while adjusting the anchor point. Once satisfied with the desired scaling, proceed to affirm your changes by clicking on the checkmark associated with the image or accessing the property bar. This action finalizes and applies the configured settings to the image within the software interface.

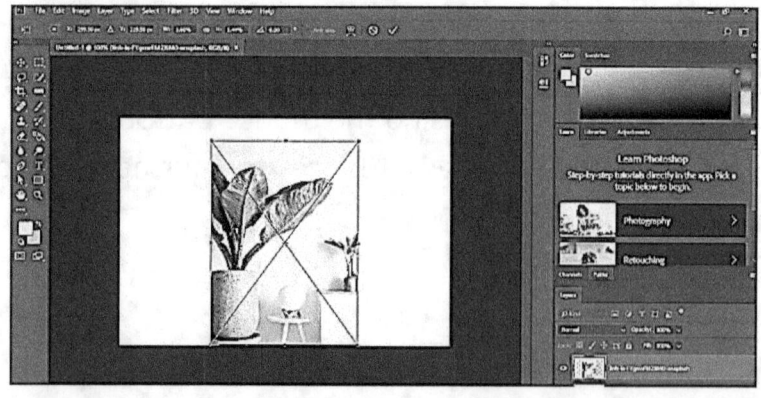

- Navigate to the Edit menu within the menu bar to access the transformative capabilities of the tool. Upon clicking the Edit menu, a dropdown list will unfold. Select the Free **Transform** option from this list by clicking on it.

- Further customization is available by delving into the Transform option, where a new dropdown list materializes. From this list, select your preferred transformation type to apply the desired changes to the image.

- You can press the Ctrl + T button from the keyboard, and once you click, a transform bounding box will appear on your image like this.
- Explore various transform properties conveniently accessible on the property bar of your image. Adjust the value of 'x' to shift the position of your image along the x-axis.

- Tailor the placement further by modifying the value of 'Y,' influencing the position of your image along the y-axis.

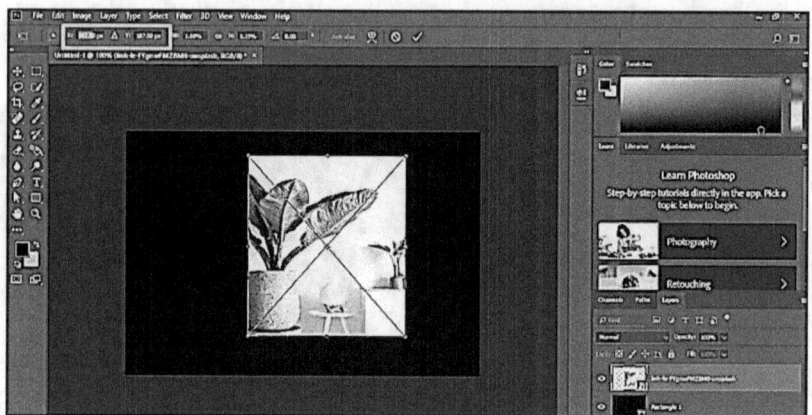

- Refine the visual aesthetics by changing the value of 'W' to adjust the width of your image.
- Elevate or diminish the height of your image by altering the value of 'H.'

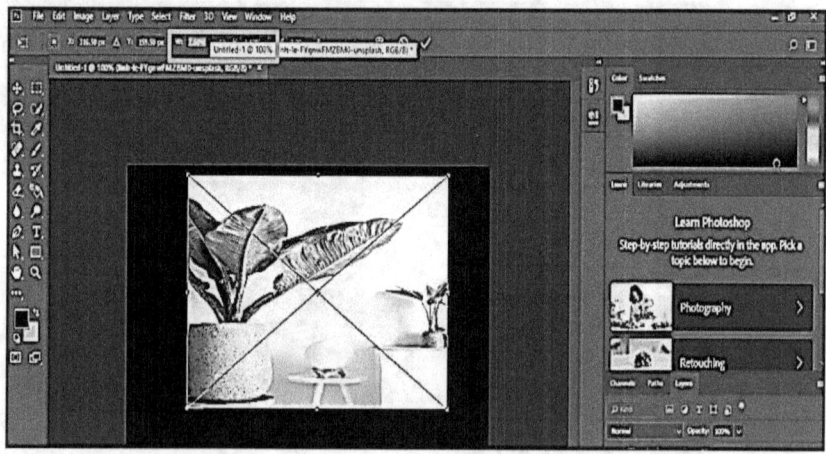

- Introduce captivating angles to your image through the 'Angle' property, facilitating smooth rotation at your desired angle.

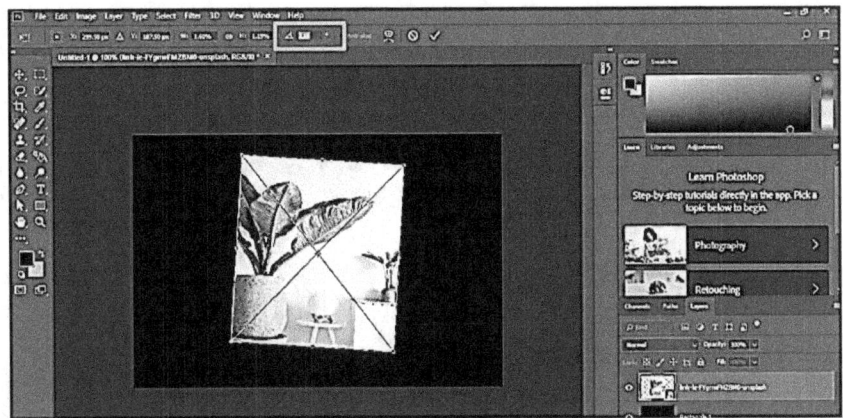

- Once satisfied with the adjustments, affirm the changes by clicking the checkmark on the property bar or simply pressing the enter button on your keyboard.
- If you decide against applying the transformation to your image, opt for the 'Cancel Transform' option or press the Esc button on your keyboard.

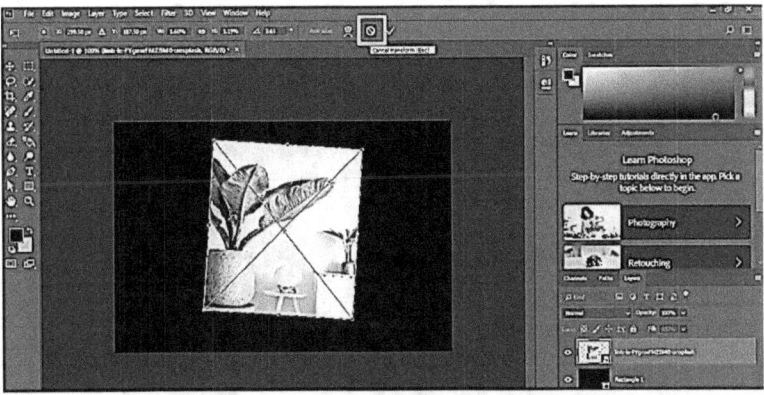

- Alternatively, streamline the transform tool by initiating a right-click on the image after pressing Ctrl + T on your keyboard. Subsequently, choose your preferred transformation option from the menu, such as scaling or rotating, to further refine your image.

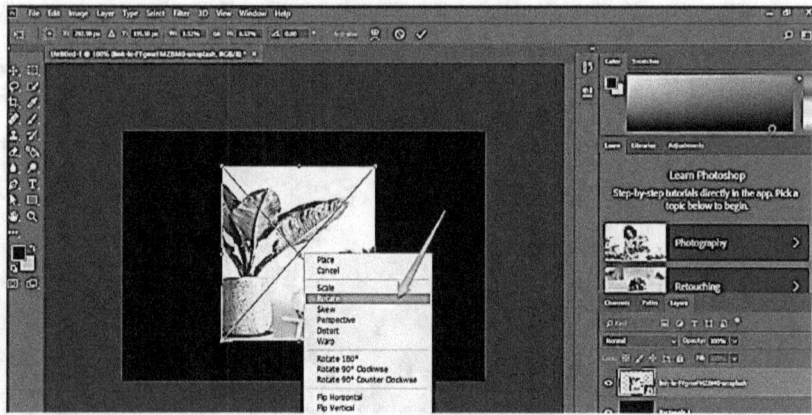

- Proceed by selecting the Skew option from the menu.

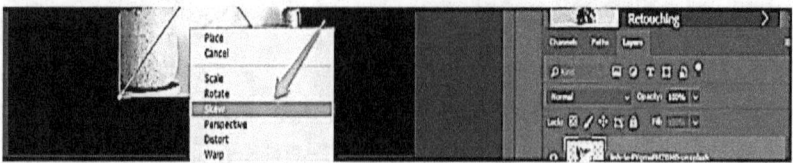

- Utilize the Skew option to reposition any anchor point of the image according to your specific requirements.

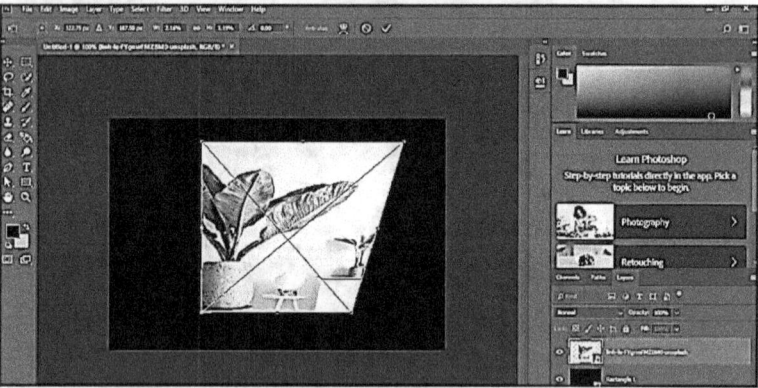

- Next, opt for the Perspective option.

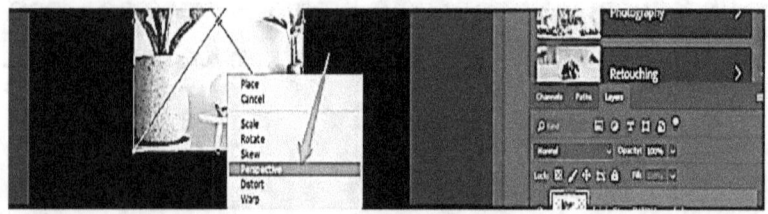

- Engage the Perspective option to observe that when you manipulate one anchor point, the corresponding anchor point on the opposite side moves in the opposite direction.

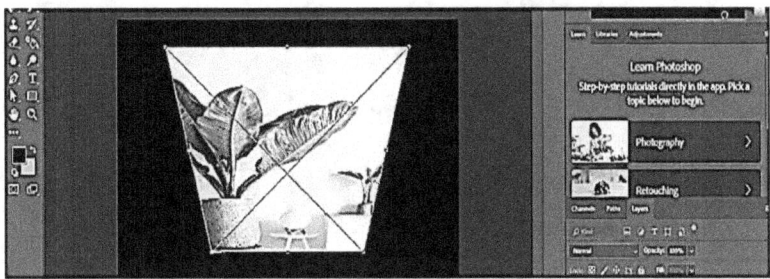

- Click on the Distort option for further adjustments.
- With the Distort option, you can manipulate the image by adjusting the bounding box lines.
- Select the Warp option from the list.

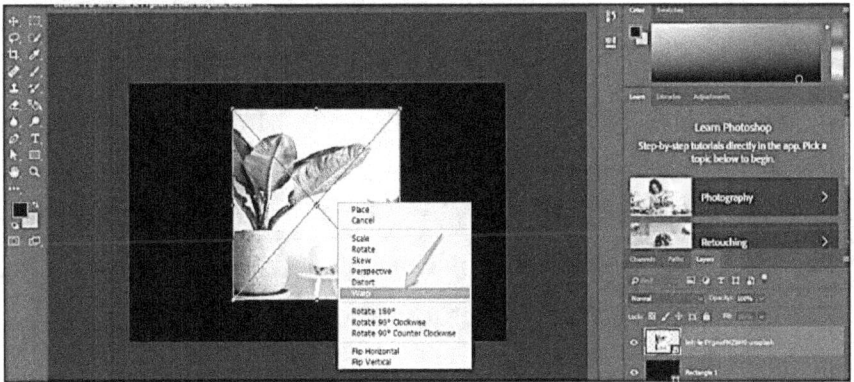

- With the Warp option, a myriad of possibilities unfolds for shaping and contouring the image. Explore the diverse transformations available through this feature to enhance the creative potential of your design.

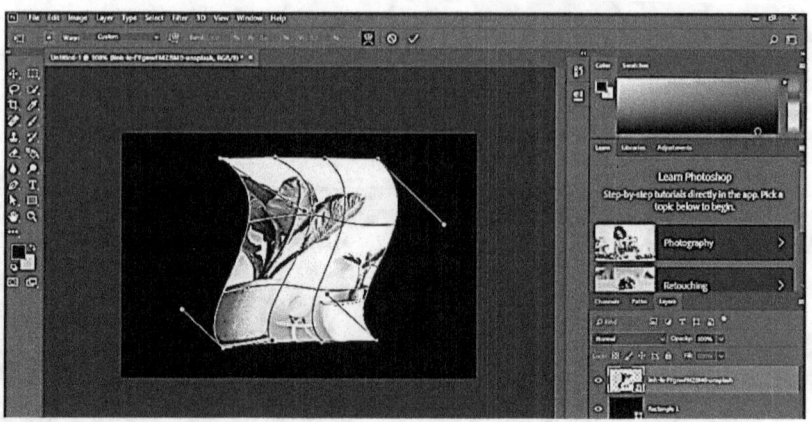

CREATE A SMOOTH TRANSITION BETWEEN IMAGES WITH A GRADIENT MASK

The upgraded Gradient Tool in the Photoshop desktop app empowers users to swiftly draw, preview, and modify captivating gradients. The improved functionality allows for the creation and editing of color stops directly from the canvas. Users gain control over various aspects, including color, density, opacity, and blend mode of the gradient. Additionally, on-canvas indicators display the mid-point and spread, facilitating precise adjustments. Multiple color stops can be added, and their colors can be easily modified, providing a comprehensive and efficient approach to gradient editing.

The Gradients feature has undergone significant enhancements, streamlining the workflow with the addition of new on-canvas controls and an automatically generated live preview that supports non-destructive editing.

To use the Gradients feature, do the following

- Click and drag on the canvas to extend the on-canvas gradient widget. While dragging, modify the gradient's angle and length.

Upon releasing the drag, revisit the gradient to further adjust the length and angle by clicking and dragging once more.

- Modify the mid-points between color stops by interacting with the diamond-shaped icons, clicking and dragging as needed.

- For removal of color stops on the on-canvas widget, select the color stop circles and drag them away from the gradient line. Alternatively, double-click the color stops (circle area) on the Gradient on-canvas widget to access the color picker for changing the color.
- Navigate to the dropdown or the Properties panel to choose a gradient preset and enhance your creative options. The live gradients in Photoshop offer a dynamic and intuitive experience for seamless editing.

Apply a gradient fill to the text

- Highlight the text you wish to fill.
- Opt for Layer > Simplify Layer to transform the vector text into a bitmap image. Note that text editing becomes disabled after simplifying the layer.

- Hold down the Control key (Command key on Mac OS) and click the thumbnail representing the text layer in the Layers panel to activate text selection.
- Choose the Gradient tool from the toolbar. Within the Tool Options bar, click the preferred gradient type. Access the Gradient Picker panel and pick a gradient fill.
- Place the cursor on the text, designating the starting point of the gradient, and drag to establish the ending point.

IMPROVE GRADIENT

Add a Layer Mask And Configure The Gradient Tool

- To incorporate a layer mask into the currently active layer, initiate the process by, Locating and clicking the "Add layer mask" button within the Layers panel. This action introduces a layer mask, a powerful tool for selectively revealing or concealing portions of the active layer.
- Following this, navigate to the Toolbar and engage the Gradient tool. Within the Options bar, refine your tool settings by opting for the Linear gradient style. It is crucial to confirm that the "Reverse colors" checkbox remains unchecked to align with the intended gradient effect.
- Delve into the intricacies of gradient customization by opening the Gradient Picker, conveniently situated in the Options bar. Here, make a deliberate selection by choosing the third gradient swatch from the left – a gradient transitioning seamlessly from black to white. This nuanced choice ensures a smooth and visually appealing gradient for your layer mask.
- Now, direct your attention to the Layers panel, where precision is key. Confirm that the layer mask thumbnail is actively selected.

You can easily identify this by the distinctive highlight border encircling the layer mask thumbnail. This step is pivotal as it designates the focus of your subsequent actions, enabling precise adjustments and enhancements to the layer mask applied to the active layer.

Gradient Tool Context Menu and Shortcuts

Confirm the appropriate context menu by utilizing shortcuts when a color stop is both selected and not selected. To unselect all color stops, a straightforward action involves clicking anywhere on the canvas.

Existing behavior	macOS	Windows	Outcome
When no color stop is selected	Control + mouse click (left/right)	Right click of the mouse	Gradients list displays
When a color stop is selected	Control + left click of the mouse	Right click of the mouse	HUD to change color
When a color stop is selected	Option + left click of the mouse	Alt + left click of the mouse	Sample to change color

HOW TO SET UP AND ALIGN THUMBNAILS IN ADOBE PHOTOSHOP

An image thumbnail serves as a compressed and scaled-down representation of its full-size counterpart. These miniature versions find versatile applications, with one of the most prevalent uses being the display of images on websites or within emails. The creation of a thumbnail in Photoshop involves a systematic process to efficiently generate a smaller-sized duplicate of the original image.

To initiate the creation of a thumbnail, start by opening the full-size image in Photoshop. Once the image is loaded, navigate to the

"Image" menu and select the "Thumbnail" command. This command effectively generates a duplicate of the image with reduced dimensions, resulting in a visually condensed version commonly referred to as a thumbnail. This resized representation is particularly useful for scenarios where showcasing the full-sized image might be impractical, such as in web design or email communication.

ADD A VARIABLE FONT TO A WEB PROJECT

What are variable fonts? Variable fonts differ from static fonts by using a single file to encompass multiple font styles, while static fonts rely on distinct files for each available style. They enable you to define a value for each design axis of a font, granting control over the font's appearance beyond the capabilities of static fonts.

Conventional static fonts necessitate the addition or installation of each individual style desired for a project. For instance, with Acumin Pro, you would typically include Acumin Pro Regular, Acumin Pro Italic, and any other preferred styles. In contrast, Acumin Variable consolidates all styles of Acumin, requiring only the addition of a single font.

Variable fonts represent a remarkably adaptable font technology. Within the Adobe Fonts variable font panel, you have the capability to tailor the appearance of these fonts and select the most suitable style for your projects. Currently, Creative Cloud applications that offer support for variable fonts include Photoshop, InDesign, and Illustrator.

How to use variable fonts on the Adobe Fonts website

To harness the capabilities of variable fonts on the Adobe Fonts website, follow these steps:

- Open your web browser and go to the Adobe Fonts website.

- Browse the available font families and identify those labeled as variable fonts.

- Click on the specific variable font family you wish to explore. This action will take you to the family detail page.

- On the family detail page, locate an interactive text tool and an accompanying panel. These tools are designed to facilitate customization.

- Use the interactive text tool to experiment with the font in real-time. Simultaneously, explore the customization options in the panel, allowing you to fine-tune various aspects of the font.

- Opt for preset instances if you want to make quick adjustments. These presets are predefined styles that showcase the font's variability.

- If you desire a more personalized touch, venture into crafting your own font style. Tweak the variables to align with your specific preferences, giving you a tailored typographic outcome.

- Once satisfied with your customizations, accept the changes by following the instructions on the page. This typically involves clicking a checkmark or a similar confirmation icon.

- Upon accepting the changes, a new editable type layer is automatically generated. This layer will be reflected in the Layers panel.

- Use the Move tool to position your customized text within the image or design.

To preserve the ability for future edits, save your project in the Photoshop (PSD) format. This ensures that the editable type layers are retained.

To leverage the dynamic capabilities of variable fonts on the Adobe Fonts website, navigate to the family detail page specific to the variable font you're interested in exploring. Here, you'll encounter a feature-rich experience, as each family detail page is thoughtfully equipped with an interactive text tool and a comprehensive panel. This combination of tools not only facilitates the exploration of the font but also empowers users with the ability to customize the font to their precise preferences.

Upon entering this space, you'll find an array of options at your disposal. The interactive text tool invites you to experiment with the font in real-time, providing a hands-on feel for the variations available. Simultaneously, the accompanying panel serves as a control center, offering a suite of customization tools.

What sets variable fonts apart is their adaptability, and this is exemplified on the Adobe Fonts website. Users can seamlessly choose from preset instances, streamlining the customization process for quick adjustments. Whether you're aiming for a bold, expressive look or a more refined and understated appearance, the preset instances provide a shortcut to achieving your desired style.

For those seeking a more tailored approach, the Adobe Fonts website offers the flexibility to craft your own font style. Dive into the nuanced adjustments, tweaking variables to align with your unique vision. This personalized customization feature ensures that your chosen variable font can be molded to suit the specific aesthetic requirements of your project.

In essence, using variable fonts on the Adobe Fonts website is not merely a functional exercise but an immersive and creative journey. It puts the power of font customization in your hands, allowing you to explore, experiment, and ultimately craft a typographic style that aligns seamlessly with your creative intent.

Enhance your photos by incorporating text.

Generate editable text using versatile Type layers.

- Access the Horizontal Type tool from the Tools panel.

- In the options bar, make selections for your text, including font, font size, color, and other preferences. Note that these settings are editable later.

- Click on the canvas to input a single line of text. Alternatively, create a text paragraph by drawing a text box and then typing within it.

- Confirm and exit text mode by clicking the check mark in the options bar. This action automatically generates a new editable type layer in the Layers panel.

- Utilize the Move tool to position your text within the image.

- Preserve the ability for future edits by saving your image in Photoshop (PSD) format, retaining the editable type layers.

WHAT IS MONITOR CALIBRATION

Calibrating a monitor or display involves adjusting its color settings to conform to the standards established by the RGB (red, green, blue) color model. Although this model originated in the nineteenth century, it remains the standard for the majority of TVs and computers. Given that nearly all screens operate on the RGB model, ensuring accurate color correction on a properly calibrated screen enhances the likelihood that your work will appear as intended on other individuals' screens.

Where to Begin Your Color Calibration

For an objectively accurate color calibration, the use of a colorimeter is essential. A colorimeter is a compact calibration device that attaches to your screen and collaborates with calibration software to fine-tune display color according to your specific screen and the ambient lighting conditions in your room. Devices like the Datacolor Spyder and the X-Rite ColorMunki can measure ambient light and provide recommended calibration settings.

Since, neither online calibration software nor the calibration tools provided by your Windows or Mac operating system are capable of achieving precise color accuracy. These programs rely on subjective assessments by the human eye, which can vary widely.

Before initiating the calibration process, allow your monitor to warm up for approximately 30 minutes. Avoid exposing your monitor to direct light, and ensure that the ambient lighting conditions mirror those under which you typically perform color adjustments to your work.

Gamma Settings: Gamma, in the context of monitor calibration, defines the rate at which shades transition from pure black to pure white. This parameter is crucial in determining the contrast within the grayscale spectrum. A higher gamma value retains the same extremes of black and white as a lower value but accentuates the contrast within that range. The choice of the recommended gamma setting is contingent upon the anticipated viewing environment for your video content. In well-lit spaces, such as offices, a gamma setting of 2.2 is advised, aligning with the standard settings for both Mac and Windows machines. Conversely, in darker settings like home theaters, a gamma setting of 2.4 is recommended, as subdued lighting enhances the visibility of contrast nuances.

Luminance: Luminance, also known as brightness, characterizes the intensity of light emitted by a screen. Maintaining consistency in luminance settings during color correction is paramount to ensure uniformity in scene adjustments. For a standard LCD screen, the recommended brightness is 120, striking a balance between vibrant visuals and comfortable viewing.

Once you have confirmed your monitor settings, the automatic calibration process takes over. Utilizing a colorimeter, this process meticulously evaluates your monitor's colors against established industry standards, charts variations, and crafts a bespoke color profile, commonly referred to as an ICC profile. With this precise profile in place, you gain the capability to pinpoint exact shades of color and ensure consistent color representation across various devices and platforms. This comprehensive calibration process contributes to a more accurate and visually satisfying viewing experience for your audience.

Recommended Frequency for Calibration

Professional colorists recommend recalibrating your displays at least once a month to maintain color consistency, particularly as monitors degrade and colors undergo changes over time.

On the other hand, some argue that technological advancements have reached a point where color reproduction on most devices is satisfactory. If achieving precise color isn't your primary concern, testing your videos across different devices can ensure there are no significant discrepancies. Director and producer Taylor Kavanaugh often adopts this approach, stating, "Our viewers are accessing our content on various devices such as iPhones, iPads, or Samsung televisions, so we always review it on all the formats we know it will be viewed on."

For those not prioritizing color accuracy, playing it safe involves avoiding extensive color adjustments. According to colorist and editor Gerry Holtz, maintaining a generic scope and keeping everything relatively balanced tends to translate well across different devices. He cautions that problems arise when pushing the boundaries, such as crushing blacks, adding excessive contrast, or oversaturating colors, as these adjustments may not translate well on diverse devices.

If issues do arise, adjustments can be made using Color Correction curves in software like Adobe Premiere Pro when editing a film shot.

ZOOMING IN PHOTOSHOP

Zoom tool

The initial approach enables you to magnify or reduce specific areas of your image by clicking on the desired region. To employ the zoom tool, either choose the icon from the toolbar or press the Z key.

The default setting for the zoom tool is to zoom in, indicated by the plus sign within the magnifying glass icon. Direct your cursor to the image and click on the area you wish to enlarge.

Click on the image as many times as you want to keep zooming in. You can also click and hold to start a continuous zoom until you release to stop the zoom.

To zoom out, select the magnifying glass icon with the minus sign in the middle from the options bar. Click anywhere on the image to zoom out, clicking as many times as needed.

You can also hold in **Alt** (Windows) or **Option** (Mac) while clicking on the image to zoom out when the zoom-in option is selected.

The zoom tool provides the ability to simultaneously zoom across all open windows in Photoshop, ensuring that each image magnifies at the same location. To enable this feature, check the box next to "Zoom All Windows."

Alternatively, by selecting the "Scrubby Zoom" option, you can click on a specific area of the image and utilize your trackpad or mouse scroll wheel to zoom in and out.

When the "Scrubby Zoom" option is not activated, you can choose an area for zooming into your image by clicking and dragging on the image. A rectangular box will appear, indicating the region where you want the image to be magnified.

Upon selecting the zoom tool, the options bar reveals three rapid zoom buttons: "100%," "Fit Screen," and "Fill Screen."

- 100% View Mode Opting for 100% will instantly magnify the image to its true size, where each pixel corresponds to one pixel on the screen. This setting allows for a detailed inspection of the image, showcasing its full intricacies. Moreover, zooming in at 100% enables an assessment of the image's clarity when printed at its actual size.

CHAPTER FOUR

HOW TO UNDO A COMMAND

Revert To The Last Saved Version

Consider this scenario: what if you find yourself needing to backtrack through multiple steps and even have the option to return to the current state? One effective method to achieve this is by reverting to the last saved version.

The prerequisite, of course, is having the foresight to create a saved version before embarking on the changes you wish to undo. Alternatively, you might desire to revert to the original image that was initially opened, making the "Revert" command particularly handy for such situations.

To execute this, navigate to the "File" option in the menu bar and select "Revert." Alternatively, you can achieve the same result by pressing F12 on the keyboard.

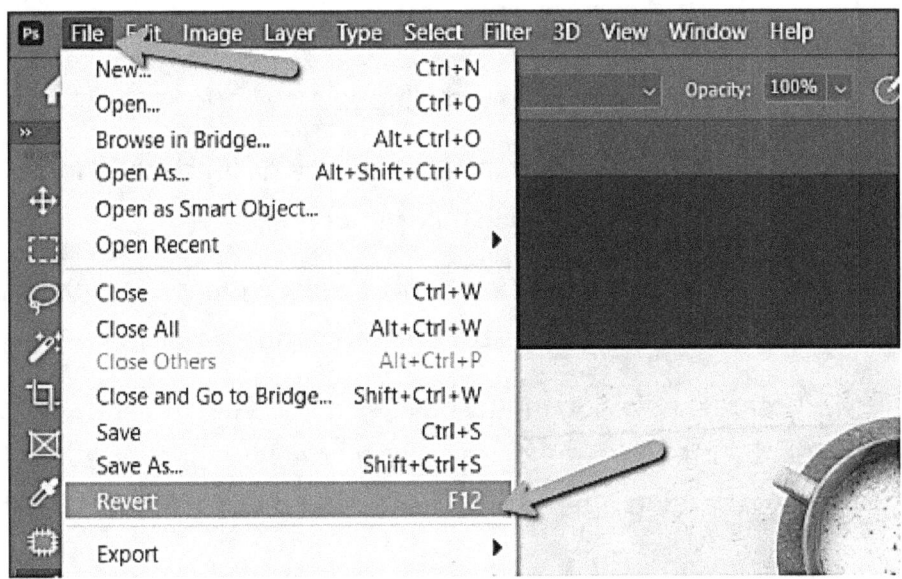

Here's the fascinating part: the "Revert" action is itself undoable. If you wish to promptly recover all the changes made before the reversion, a simple press of Ctrl + Z (Command + Z) allows you to undo the "Revert" command seamlessly.

Boom! This functionality adds a layer of flexibility and control to your editing process, providing a quick and efficient means to navigate through changes and revert when needed.

MAKING USE OF THE HISTORY PANEL

Harness the power of the History panel in Illustrator to seamlessly navigate through various stages of your design during your current working session. As you introduce new elements to your design, each addition manifests as a distinct state within the History panel.

For instance, actions such as selection, pen tool drawing, and rotation of design components are cataloged individually in the panel. Upon selecting a specific state, your artwork reverts to its appearance when that particular change was initially applied, providing a foundation for further modifications.

Follow these steps to access and leverage the History panel:

1. Open the History panel by choosing Window > History.

2. To undo a specific change, select the desired state and click "Step Backward" from the History panel menu.

3. For redoing a specific change, select the state and click "Step Forward" from the History panel menu.

4. Create a new document based on the selected state by choosing it in the History panel and clicking [Include the symbol representing a new document creation].

5. To adjust the number of states visible in the History panel, click "Set History Limit" from the History panel menu. Choose the desired number of states from the History States menu.

6. If you wish to eliminate states that follow a selected state, choose the state in the History panel and click "Clear History" from the History panel menu.

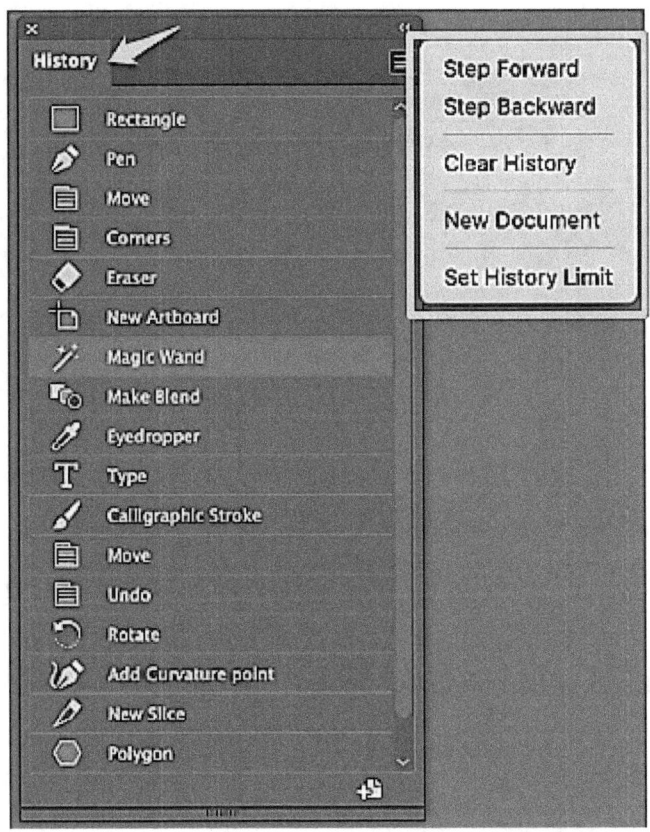

Mastering the History panel allows you to fluidly navigate the evolution of your design, facilitating precise control over undoing, redoing, and branching into new creative directions within your Illustrator project.

Crop a photo

- Choose the Crop Tool Select the crop tool icon from the left toolbar—it resembles a square with overlapping corners—or simply press the C key, a logical keyboard shortcut in Photoshop. Upon selection, a bounding box appears over the photograph, featuring white borders at the corners and midpoints, visually indicating the size and shape of the impending crop.

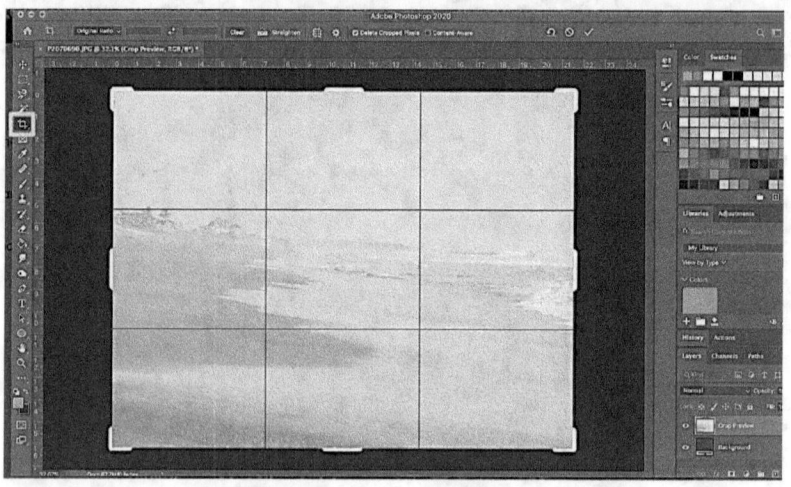

- Opt for an Aspect Ratio (Optional) By default, Photoshop adheres to the original aspect ratio of the photo or the last aspect ratio you selected with the crop tool. If you desire a specific shape, such as an 8×10 for printing or a square for Instagram, you'll need to adjust the aspect ratio.

Navigate to the drop-down menu at the top (defaulted to "original ratio") and select the desired ratio. For instance, 1:1 signifies a square, while 4:5 replicates the proportions of an 8 x 10-inch print.

If you prefer a more flexible approach without being confined to a specific aspect ratio, utilize the "clear" button on the top toolbar for an unrestricted crop tool.

- Adjust Size Resize the crop box by manipulating its corners until it encompasses only the elements you wish to include in the photo. Additionally, you can click and hold in the middle of the crop box to reposition it around the photograph, altering the framing while maintaining the same overall size.
- Straighten (Optional) While the crop box is active, position the mouse pointer over the outer corner until the curved, double-headed arrow appears. Click and drag to rotate the crop box, aligning it for a straightened image.

Alternatively, access the straighten tool from the top menu. Draw a line across a straight element in the photo, like the horizon. Upon drawing the line, Photoshop automatically straightens the image. This step is discretionary if your photo is already aligned but serves as a swift solution for correcting a skewed horizon.

- Confirm the Crop To complete the cropping process, press the Enter key. However, before doing so, consider deselecting the "Delete Cropped Pixels" option from the top toolbar. If left unchecked, finalizing the crop would result in irreversible changes, limiting your ability to revisit and modify it. Unlike in Lightroom, Photoshop's default cropping is inherently destructive, so it's advisable to keep "Delete Cropped Pixels" off unless you are certain that no further adjustments will be needed.

How to manipulate the perspective of an image using Perspective Warp

Follow this tutorial on using Photoshop's Perspective Warp to make adjustments to the perspective in your photos.

Begin by opening and preparing the image

Once your file is open in Photoshop, choose the layer you wish to modify. If your image is on the background layer, duplicate it to another layer to avoid permanent pixel loss in the original image. This allows you to retain the option to revert to the original. Click on "Layer" › "Duplicate Layer" in the top menu.

Select and mask the object for adjustment

Proceed to Step 4 if you intend to use Perspective Warp on the entire image. For adjusting a specific object, continue with Step 2. If you want your edits to affect only one object, create a mask around it using one of Photoshop's Selection tools. Then, click on "Select and Mask" in the options bar.

Create a Smart Object

Convert the layer mask into a Smart Object for nondestructive and reversible edits. Select the layer mask in the Layers panel, then choose "Layer" › "Smart Object" › "Create Smart Object" from the top menu.

Access the Perspective Warp tool

Choose "Edit" › "Perspective Warp" from the top menu. If the feature is not accessible, enable the graphics processor by clicking on "Photoshop" › "Preferences" › "Performance" in the top menu. Select "Use Graphics Processor" in the Graphics Processor Settings.

Define the planes of your image

Click and drag to create quads along the planes of the architecture or objects you want to shift. Ensure the edges are parallel to the straight lines in the image. Corners snap together when dragged close to each other.

Adjust the planes

Switch to Warp mode in the options bar. Move the object and alter the perspective. Use automatic buttons to level horizontal or vertical lines, or both. Adjust the corners of the quads to your desired positions. For instance, shift the perspective of a building by shortening one side or lengthening the other.

- Maintain straight lines. Shift-click to make a line vertical, moving an entire side instead of just a corner. Shift-click multiple lines to keep them straight while moving. Once satisfied with changes, click the checkmark in the options bar to close Perspective Warp.

- Crop or fill in the background. Perspective Warp may result in pixel loss at the frame edges. Correct this by selecting the Crop tool and shrinking the frame. Alternatively, use the Healing Brush or Clone Stamp tool to fill in missing pixels. Option-click (Mac) or Alt-click (Windows) to copy an area, then click on the area with missing pixels. Ensure the "Select All Layers" option is checked in the option bar for both tools.

HOW TO ADJUST THE CANVAS SIZE

The initial approach involves navigating to the Menu bar, selecting "Image," and opting for "Canvas Size." Alternatively, you can utilize the keyboard shortcut Alt + Ctrl + C (Option + Command + C on a Mac) to access the command.

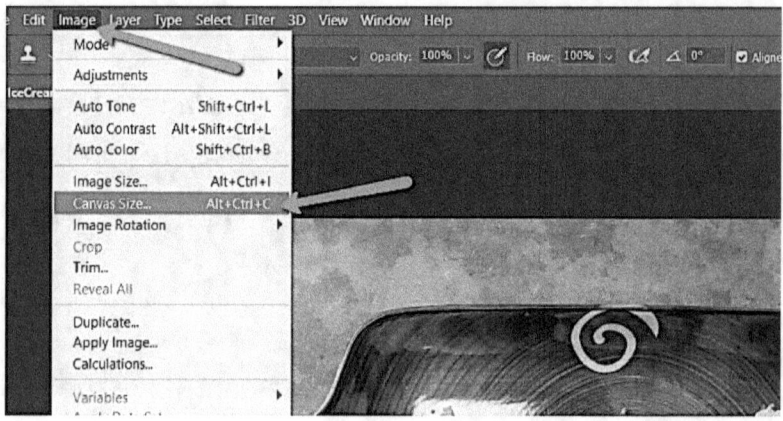

Ensure that you specifically choose "Canvas Size" and not "Image Size." Selecting "Image Size" will alter the dimensions of the image itself, potentially distorting or damaging pixels. On the other hand, "Canvas Size" adjusts the dimensions of the canvas on which the image is positioned, leaving the image unaffected.

In the ensuing panel, designate the new width and height, which can be expressed in various units such as pixels, inches, points, and more, as illustrated in the dropdown menu.

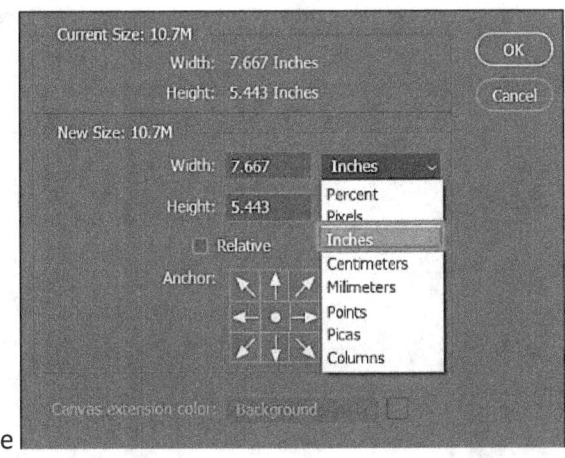

e

Now, the next step is to select an anchor point. Opt for the central circle to center the image, or choose any of the corresponding arrows to position the image in one of the corners, sides, top, or bottom.

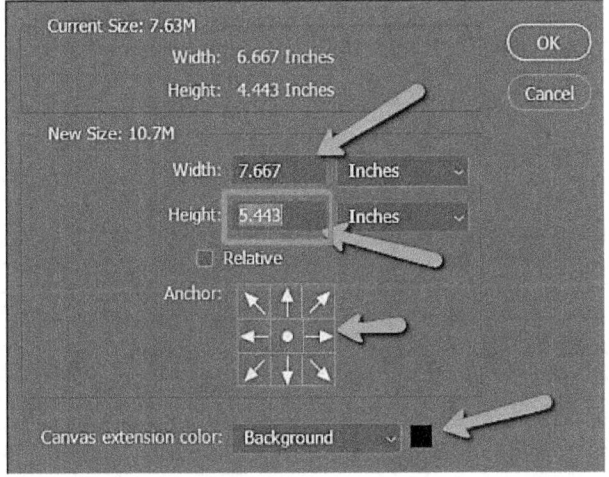

Towards the bottom of the panel, you can also specify the color of the canvas. For instance, in my case, I opted for black. Once you've made your selections, click OK, and you'll observe a black border surrounding my image.

HOW TO ADD PHOTOS AS LAYER DESIGN

Drag and drop

Locate the desired image on your computer. After selecting your image, drag and drop it into your currently open Photoshop project. Subsequently, the image will be positioned onto your canvas and will manifest as a new layer in the Layers Panel.

Now, you have the flexibility to scale or reposition the image according to your preferences. If resizing, rotating, or transforming the image is on your agenda, activate the Move Tool (V) first. Subsequently, press Control + T (Win) or Command + T (Mac) to activate the Transform Tool. Use the handles of the transform box to resize the image to your liking.

Once satisfied with the adjustments, press the Enter key on your keyboard or click the checkmark in the Options Bar. Your image will then be integrated into the existing layer above your original image, residing on its dedicated layer.

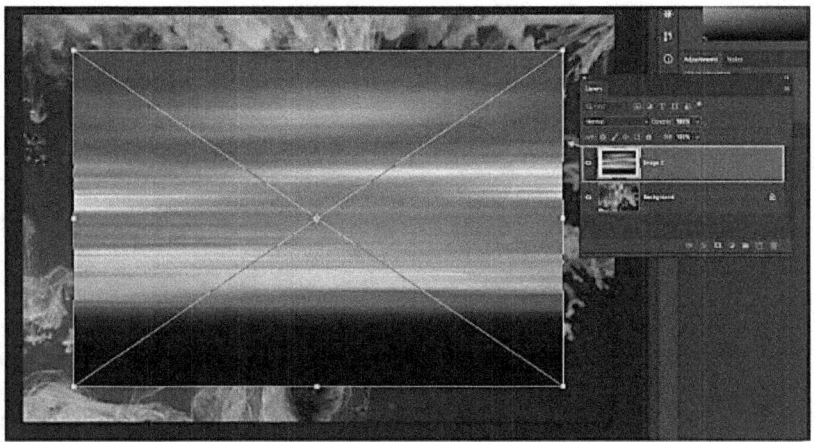

Place and embedded or linked object

- This approach allows you to find and incorporate an image

from your Hard Drive.

Initiate the process by opening the document where you wish to insert the image. Then, navigate to File > Place Embedded.

- Locate the image file on your device, select it, and click "Place" located at the bottom of the panel.

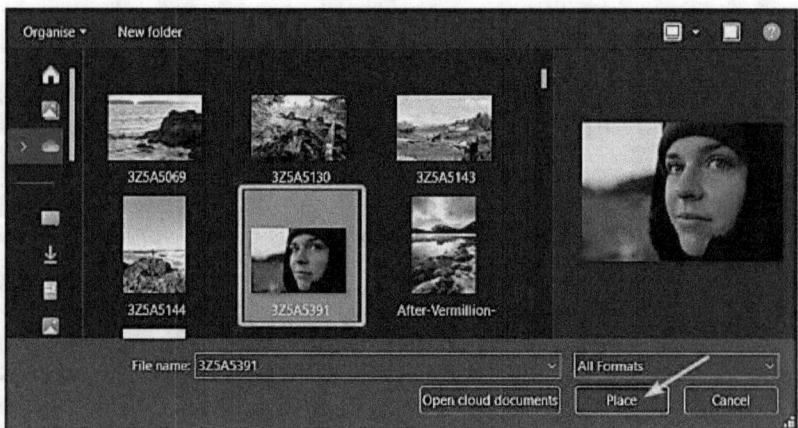

- If necessary, you can resize and reposition the image. Start by activating the Move Tool (V) from the Toolbar, followed by the Transform Tool using Control + T (Win) or Command + T (Mac). Employ the transform box to adjust the position and size of the image.
- Press Enter to confirm the changes.

Copy and paste

Another alternative at your disposal is the straightforward copy-and-paste method. This approach is particularly effective when dealing with images already open in Photoshop but across different projects.

Begin by selecting the image you intend to copy. Proceed to Edit >
Copy or use the keyboard shortcut Control + C (Win) or Command +
C (Mac).

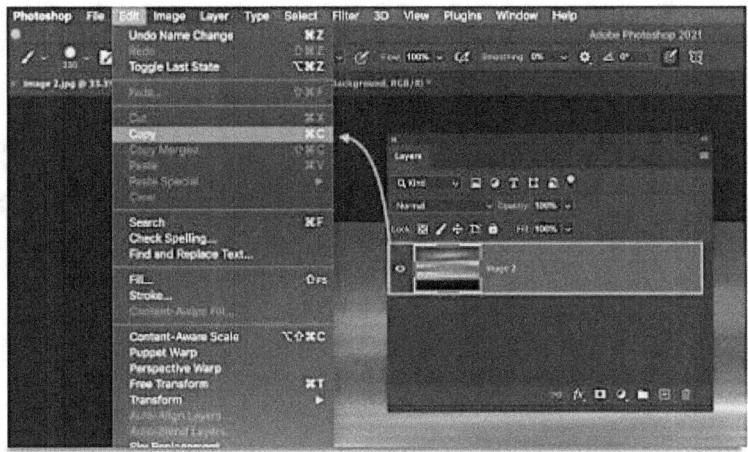

Transitioning to your alternative project, navigate to Edit > Paste or
use the keyboard shortcut Control + V (Win) or Command + V (Mac).

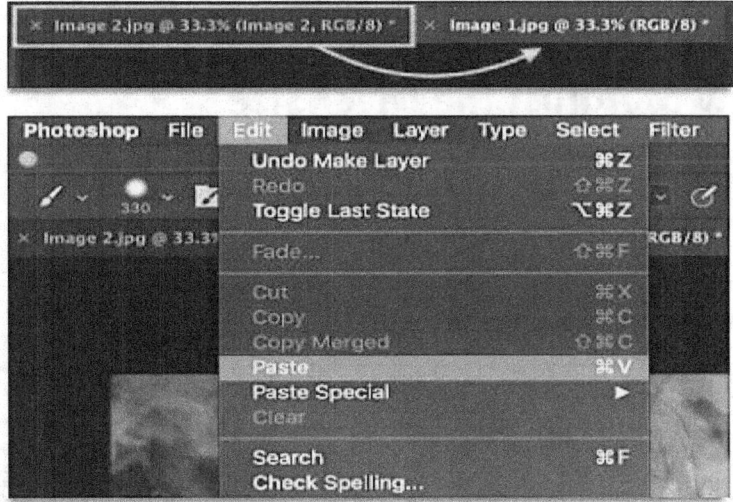

Upon pasting, your copied image assumes the form of a new layer in
your secondary project. Utilize the Move Tool (V) to both resize and
reposition it according to your preferences.

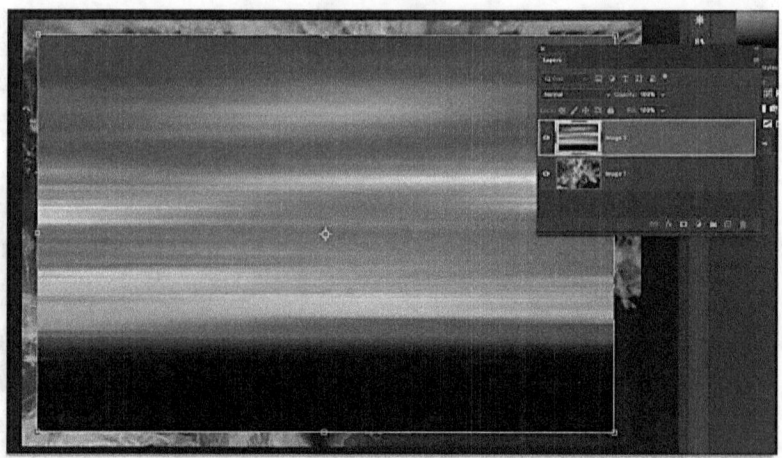

Now, you face the decision of whether to maintain the images as separate entities or combine them into one. Generally, leaving them on distinct layers is advisable for enhanced adjustment options down the line.

If merging the layers aligns with your intentions, execute this by pressing Control + E (Win) or Command + E (Mac).

How to Adjust the Layer Size

1. Choose the layer you wish to adjust, located in the "Layers" panel on the right side of the screen.

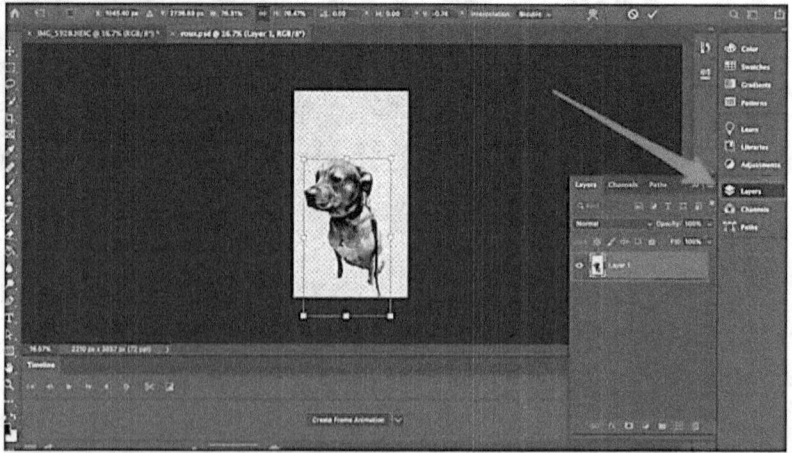

2. Navigate to "Edit" on the top menu bar and select "Free Transform." The resizing bars will appear over the layer.

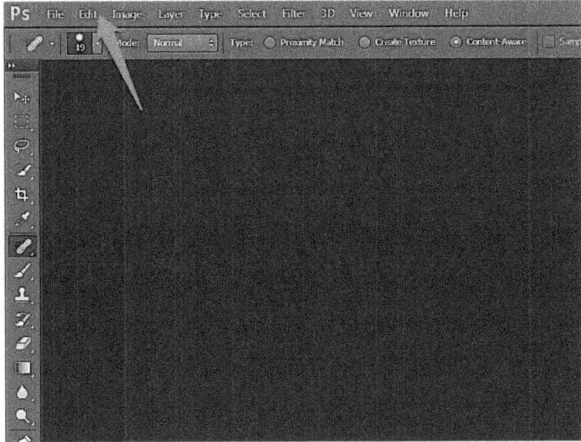

3. Adjust the layer to your desired size by dragging and dropping. To maintain proportions, hold down the shift key while dragging to manipulate both height and width.

The checkmark in the top options bar will no longer be visible and has slightly larger fonts. Remember to press Ctrl or Command+S to save your work as you progress.

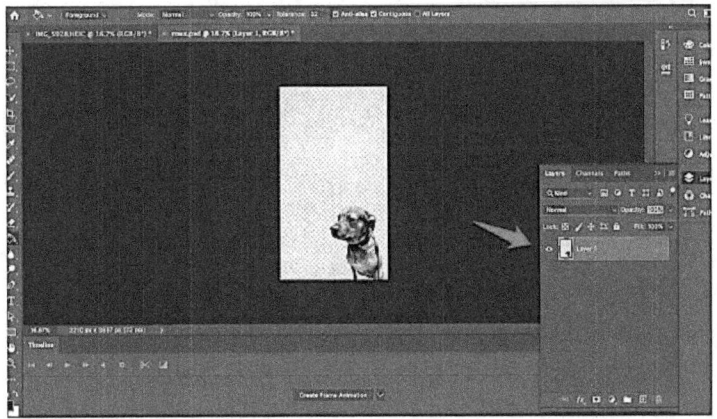

4. Confirm the changes by selecting the checkmark in the top options bar. When you hover over the checkmark, the words "Commit transform (enter)" will appear. Alternatively, you can

press Enter for Windows or Return for macOS to finalize the resizing.

How to Adjust Brightness And Contrast

Here's an image currently open in Photoshop. While not bad, it could benefit from an enhancement in brightness and contrast. Let's explore how a Brightness/Contrast adjustment layer can achieve this improvement without permanently altering any pixels in the image.

In the past, when applying Brightness/Contrast as a static adjustment, we had to create a copy of the image and place it on a new layer to avoid modifying the original image. However, with adjustment layers, this step is unnecessary as they are entirely non-destructive. To add one, there are various methods, one of which involves navigating to the Layer menu in the Menu Bar at the top of the screen, selecting New Adjustment Layer, and then opting for Brightness/Contrast

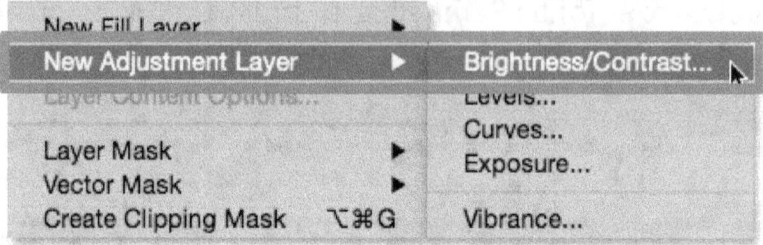

An alternative method is to select the Brightness/Contrast icon from Photoshop's Adjustments panel. Positioned as the first icon on the left in the top row, you can identify each adjustment layer by hovering your mouse cursor over the icons

If the Adjustments panel is not visible on your screen, access it by going to the Window menu. Here, you'll find a list of all available panels in Photoshop. Choose Adjustments, and a checkmark next to the name indicates that the panel is currently open. If not, locate it (by default, it may be nested with the Styles panel or, as of CC 2014, with the Styles and Libraries panels). If there's no checkmark, select the Adjustments panel to open it

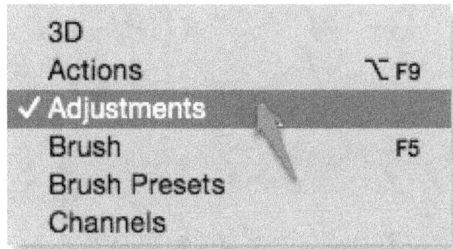

The preferred method I often use for adding a Brightness/Contrast adjustment layer involves clicking on the New Fill or Adjustment Layer icon located at the bottom of the Layers panel.

To implement this, click on the New Fill or Adjustment Layer icon in the Layers panel.

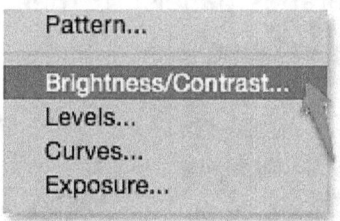

Subsequently, choose Brightness/Contrast from the provided list. Initially, there will be no visible change to the image, but a new Brightness/Contrast adjustment layer will appear above the image in the Layers panel.

- Click on the Auto button. Unlike applying Brightness/Contrast as a static adjustment, where options and controls are presented in a separate dialog box, adjustment layers reveal these settings in the Properties panel, introduced to Photoshop in CS6. In this panel, you'll find familiar controls such as the Brightness and Contrast sliders, the Auto button, and the Use Legacy option, all of which were extensively covered in the preceding tutorial.

As with previous steps, our initial action typically involves clicking the Auto button. This prompts Photoshop to analyze your image in comparison to those of other professional photographers, aiming to determine the optimal brightness and contrast settings

In my instance, Photoshop opted for a Brightness setting of 54 and a Contrast setting of 66. It's important to note that each image is distinct, so if you're working with your own photo, the likelihood is that these values will vary.

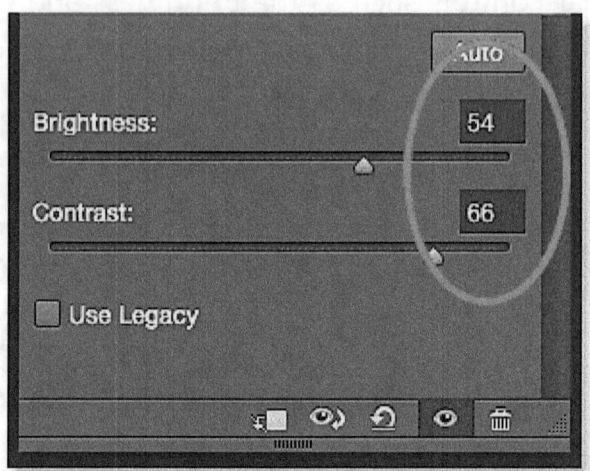

- Fine-Tune with the Brightness and Contrast Sliders If you find that the Auto button adjustments are not quite perfect for your image, you have the option to refine it further using the Brightness and Contrast sliders. Moving a slider to the right enhances brightness or contrast while dragging it to the left reduces brightness or contrast.

  While I generally appreciate the adjustments made by Photoshop, I've decided to make a slight modification to suit my personal taste for this particular image. I'll decrease the Brightness value to around 45 and increase the Contrast to 75. It's important to note that these adjustments reflect my individual preference for this specific image. As you work with your photo, keep a close eye on the document to fine-tune the sliders and find the settings that best complement your vision.

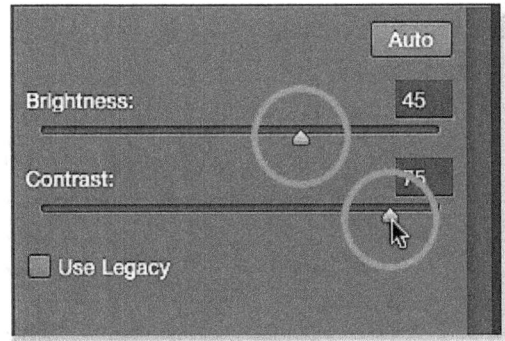

Here's the application of manual adjustments. For comparison, the original, untouched version is displayed on the left, while the modified version is showcased on the right

The Option of "Using Legacy"

Exploring the "Use Legacy" Option Similar to the static iteration of the Brightness/Contrast command, the adjustment layer version incorporates a "Use Legacy" option. This option directs the Brightness/Contrast command to operate in the manner it did prior to Photoshop CS3. While I won't delve extensively into it here, as it was thoroughly discussed in the previous tutorial, a quick reminder (especially for those who haven't yet perused the earlier tutorial): I'll click inside the checkbox to select the "Use Legacy" option (it is initially deactivated).

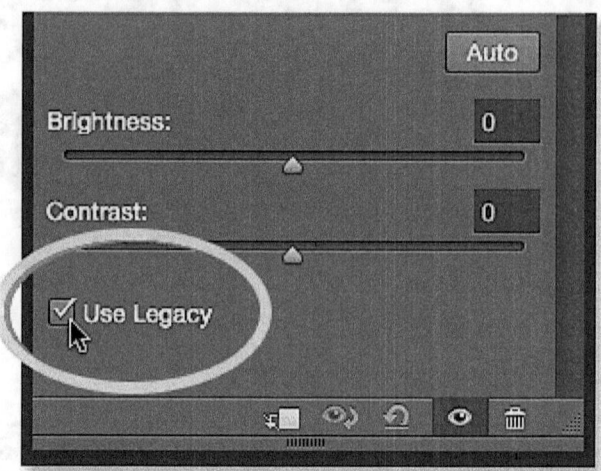

Enabling the "Use Legacy" option instructs the Brightness/Contrast command to emulate its behavior from the era before Photoshop CS3, a time when Adobe implemented significant enhancements. In the versions preceding CS3 (such as CS2), Brightness/Contrast was notorious for its limited capabilities and was often associated with image deterioration. As a brief illustration, with "Use Legacy" activated, I'll pull both the Brightness and Contrast sliders to their maximum values by dragging them all the way to the right. This action results in a completely overexposed image, accompanied by peculiar color artifacts. The outcome stems from Photoshop merely pushing the pixels in the image to extremes, causing lighter tones to transition to pure white and darker tones to shift to pure black.

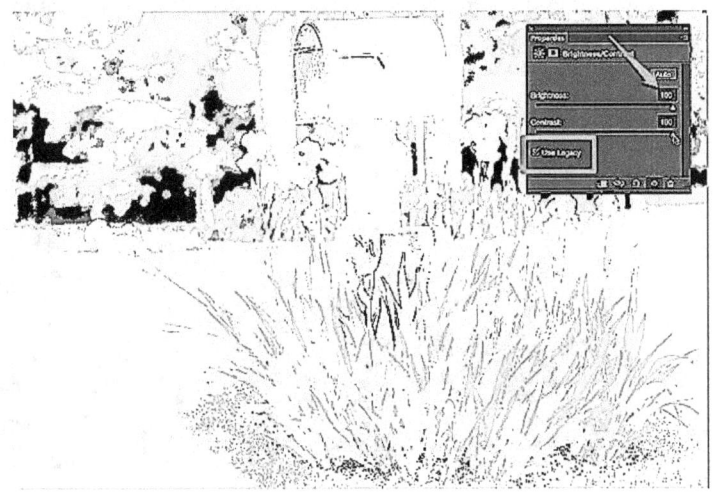

In contrast, when the Brightness and Contrast are both increased, the image becomes excessively bright; however, without enabling the Use Legacy option, it manages to preserve the majority of its details.

Similarly, when I re-activate the Use Legacy option and move both the Brightness and Contrast sliders to the left, minimizing them to their lowest values, the result is not just an excessively dark image but one that entirely lacks any remaining detail.

When the Use Legacy option is deactivated, reducing both Brightness and Contrast maintains the majority of the image's details. In contemporary settings, there's generally no need to activate the Use Legacy option unless you specifically aim to compare the older version of Brightness/Contrast with its improved functionality today. Since it is disabled by default, it is advisable to leave it in that state.

CHAPTER FIVE

HOW TO ADJUST COLOR VIBRANCY

To enhance or tone down color vibrancy in Photoshop version 2024, utilize the Vibrance adjustment layer with the following steps:

1. Open the desired image for editing in Photoshop version 2024.

2. In the menu bar, navigate to Layer > New Adjustment Layer > Vibrance. Alternatively, you can click the Vibrance icon in the Adjustments panel or choose Image > Adjustments > Vibrance.

3. In the Properties panel, adjust the Vibrance slider to intensify or diminish color saturation, ensuring minimal color clipping during saturation increases.

4. To target less saturated colors for more adjustment and avoid color clipping at full saturation, slide the Vibrance slider to the right. For uniform saturation adjustment across all colors, regardless of their initial saturation levels, use the Saturation slider. To decrease saturation, shift either the Vibrance or Saturation slider to the left.

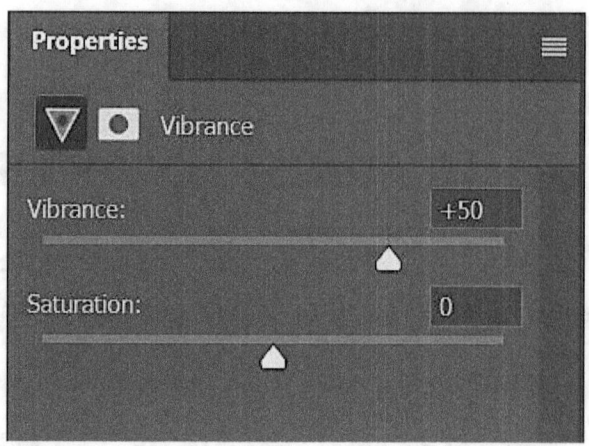

The Vibrance adjustment layer optimizes saturation to minimize clipping as colors approach maximum saturation. It accentuates less-saturated colors more than already vibrant ones. Additionally, Vibrance helps prevent skin tones from becoming overly saturated.

How To Modifying The Saturation And Hue

The Hue/Saturation command allows for the adjustment of hue (color), saturation (purity), and lightness across the entire image or individual color components within an image.

Employ the Hue slider to introduce special effects, colorize a black-and-white image (such as applying a sepia effect), or alter the spectrum of colors within a specific section of an image.

A. Original

B. Complete transformation of the entire image to sepia utilizing the Colorize option

C. Targeted adjustment of magenta colors through the Edit menu using the Hue slider

A   B   C

Employ the Saturation slider to enhance or diminish the vibrancy of colors. For instance, you can intensify the colors in a landscape to add vibrancy or tone down a distracting color, such as a vivid red sweater in a portrait.

1. Changing the saturation or Hue, either pattern is followed

   - Navigate to Enhance > Adjust Color > Adjust Hue/Saturation.

   - Opt for Layer > New Adjustment Layer > Hue/Saturation, or access an existing Hue/Saturation adjustment layer.

Within the dialog box, observe two color bars representing the colors in their sequence on the color wheel. The upper bar displays the color before adjustment, while the lower bar illustrates the impact of the adjustment on all hues at full **saturation.**

2. In the Edit drop-down menu, select the colors to modify:

   - Opt for Master to adjust all colors simultaneously.

   - Choose from the preset color ranges listed for the color requiring adjustment. An adjustment slider will appear between the color bars, enabling you to edit specific ranges of hues.

3. For adjusting Hue, input a value or manipulate the slider until the colors align with your preferences. The values in the text box signify the degree of rotation around the color wheel from the pixel's

113

original color. A positive value indicates clockwise rotation, while a negative value indicates counterclockwise rotation, ranging from −180 to +180.

4. To modify Saturation, input a value or slide the slider to the right for increased saturation or left for decreased saturation. Values range from −100 to +100.

5. For Lightness adjustments, input a value or slide the slider to the right for increased lightness or left for decreased lightness. Exercise caution when using this slider on an entire image, as it may reduce the tonal range of the overall image.

6. Click OK. To cancel changes and start anew, hold down Alt (Option in Mac OS) and click Reset.

APPLY A HUE/ SATURATION ADJUSTMENT

To apply an adjustment layer either method adopted:

- In the menu bar, navigate to Layer > New Adjustment Layer > Hue/Saturation, and click OK in the New Layer dialog box.

- In the Adjustments panel, click the Hue/Saturation icon.

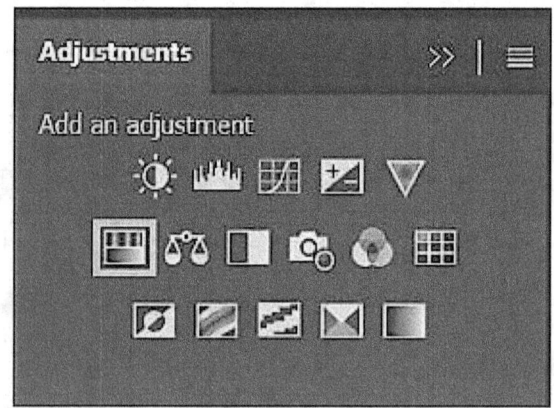

Alternatively, you can opt for Image > Adjustments > Hue/Saturation, but be aware that this method directly modifies the image layer and discards image information.

In the Properties panel, follow these steps:

- Choose a Hue/Saturation preset from the Preset menu.

- From the menu next to the On-image adjustment tool:

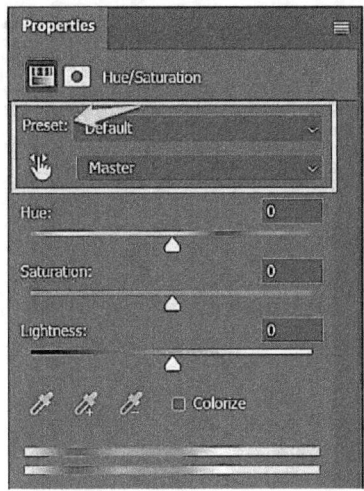

- Choose Master to adjust all colors simultaneously.

- Select one of the preset color ranges listed for the color requiring adjustment. For customizing the color range, refer to Specify the range of colors adjusted using Hue/Saturation.

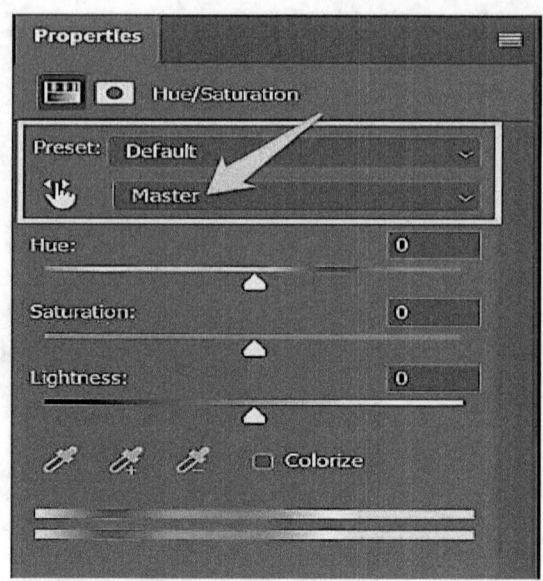

To modify the hue

- Drag the Hue slider or input a value until you achieve the desired colors.

- The values in the box indicate the degree of rotation around a color wheel from the original pixel color, with positive values indicating clockwise rotation and negative values indicating counterclockwise rotation (ranging from -180 to +180).

- Alternatively, use the On-image adjustment tool. Ctrl-click (Windows) or Command-click (Mac OS) a color in the image and drag left or right to adjust the Hue value.

For adjusting saturation

- Input a value or slide the Saturation slider to the right for increased saturation or left for decreased saturation.

- Values range from -100 (indicating desaturation, resulting in duller colors) to +100 (indicating increased saturation).

To adjust lightness

- Enter a value or slide the Lightness slider to the right to increase lightness (adding white to a color) or left to decrease it (adding black to a color).

- Values range from -100 (percentage of black) to +100 (percentage of white).

To revert a Hue/Saturation setting, click the reset button at the bottom of the Properties panel.

Specify the range of colors adjusted with the use of Hue/Saturation

1. Apply a Hue/Saturation adjustment.
2. In the Properties panel, select a color from the menu adjacent to the On-image adjustment button.

Specify the color range, and observe the adjustment sliders along with their corresponding color wheel values (in degrees) situated between the two color bars.

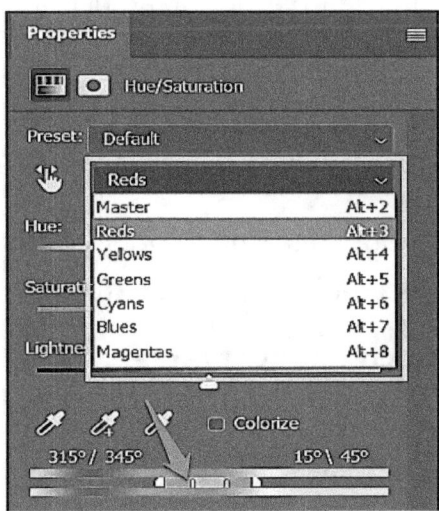

- The inner vertical sliders define the color range.

- The outer triangle sliders indicate where adjustments on a color range taper off (fall-off, referring to a gradual feathering of adjustments instead of a sharply defined on/off application).

To modify the range of colors, utilize either the eyedropper tools or the adjustment sliders

- Click or drag in the image using the Eyedropper tool to choose a color range.

- To expand the range, click or drag with the Add To Sample Eyedropper tool.

- To narrow the range, click or drag with the Subtract From Sample Eyedropper tool.

- While an eyedropper tool is selected, press Shift to add to the range or Alt (Windows) or Option (Mac OS) to subtract from it.

Adjust the color fall-off

- Drag one of the white triangle sliders to control the amount of color fall-off (feathering of adjustment) without affecting the range.

- Adjust the range without impacting the fall-off by dragging the area between the triangle and the vertical bar.

- Move the entire adjustment slider (including triangles and vertical bars) to select a different color area by dragging the center area.

Refine the color component range

- Drag one of the vertical white bars to modify the range of the color component. Moving a vertical bar closer to a triangle and away from the center increases the color range and decreases the fall-off. Moving a vertical bar toward the center and away from a triangle decreases the color range and increases the fall-off.

- Ctrl-drag (Windows) or Command-drag (Mac OS) the color bar to reposition a different color in the center of the bar.

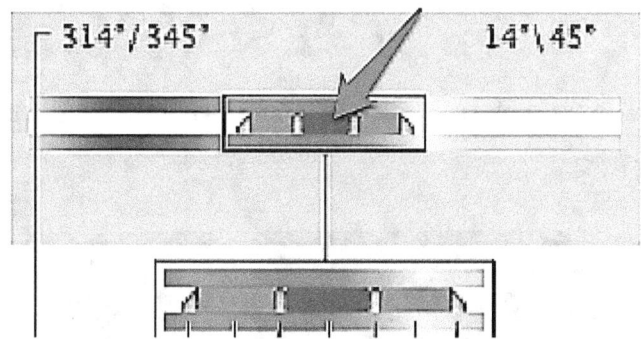

How To Change The Color Of A Shape Layer In Photoshop

To modify the color of a shape layer in Photoshop, begin by choosing your shape layer and activating the Shape Tool (U). Navigate to the upper settings bar, where you should click on the "Fill" option. From the available swatches, pick a new color, and the chosen color will be applied to the shape, thereby changing its color.

Let's delve into more detail.

If you haven't created a shape layer yet, start by selecting one of the Shape Tools (U). Click and drag on your canvas to generate a new shape.

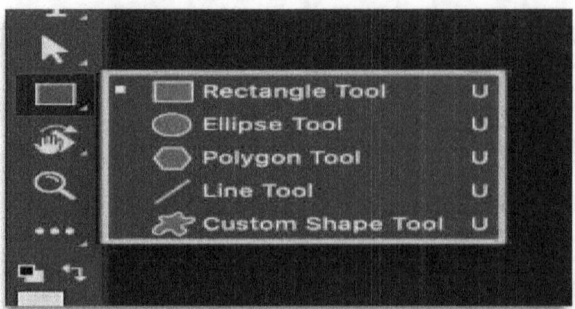

Ensure that the shape layer is now chosen in the Layers Panel.

While the Shape Tool is active, navigate to the upper settings bar and select the "Fill" option. The fill setting determines the color of any shape layer you're working with in Photoshop.

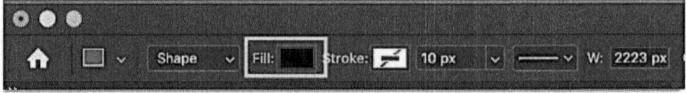

In the fill panel that emerges, you have the option to pick from preset swatches for swift color adjustments.

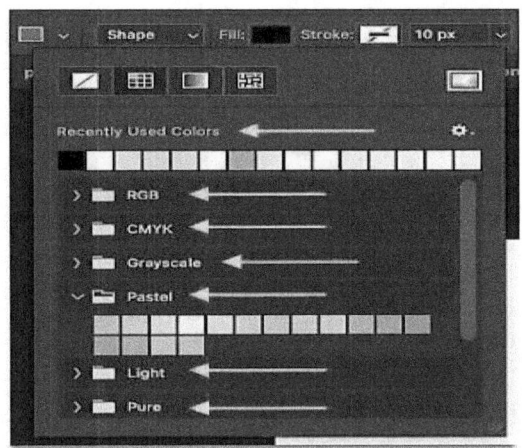

For a more precise color change to your shape layer, click on the color picker icon in the right corner. Within the color picker, manually choose a new color by selecting from the color palette. Once you're satisfied with the color, click OK to apply the color change to your shape.

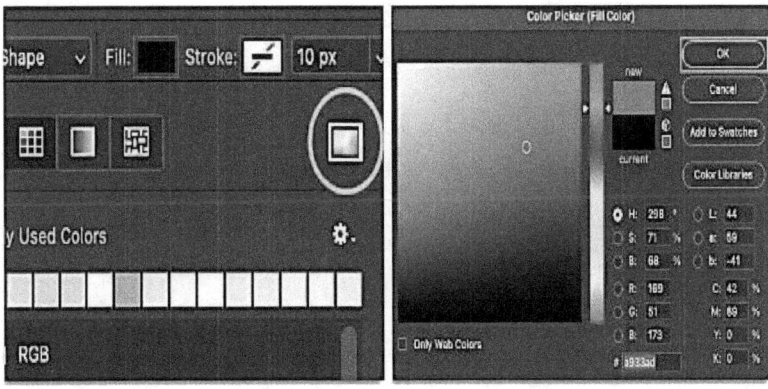

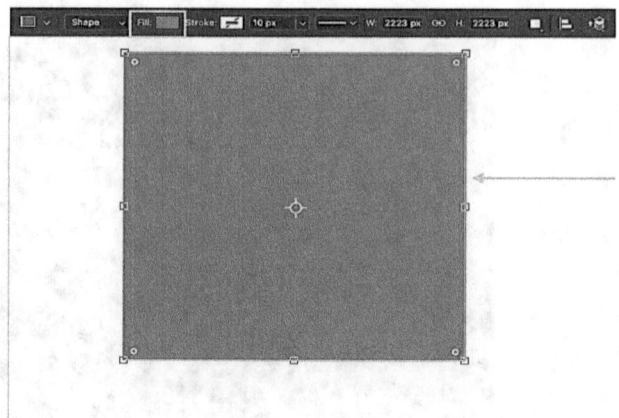

And just like that, you've efficiently altered the color of a shape layer in Photoshop! However, there's much more to explore when it comes to changing the color of shapes, extending beyond basic solid colors.

Changing the Color of the Background Layer in Photoshop

When initiating a new project in Photoshop, the starting point is often the background layer, which typically defaults to white. However, if you wish to personalize it with a custom color, you can explore two methods based on whether you're starting a new project or working on an existing one.

Modifying the Background Color for a New Project

Within the new document dialogue box, you have the flexibility to customize dimensions, resolution, and even the background layer color before its creation. In the "Background Contents" option, you can choose from five different background options:

1. White

2. Black

3. Background Color (reflecting your currently active background color in the Photoshop workspace)

4. Transparent

5. Custom

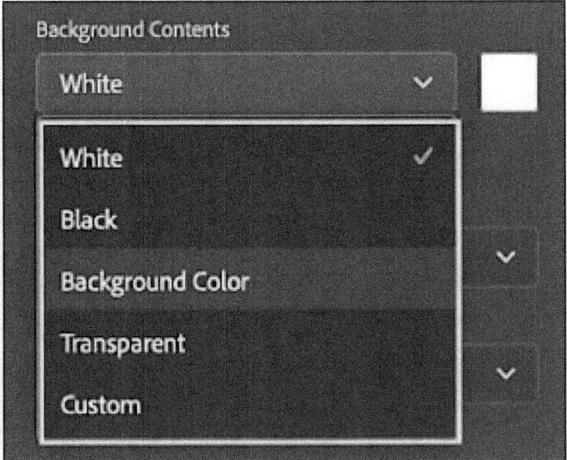

Most of these choices are quite straightforward, so simply pick the background color that suits your preference. If the desired color is not available, click on "Custom" and select a color from the appearing color palette. With these straightforward options, you can modify the background layer color before your project comes into existence.

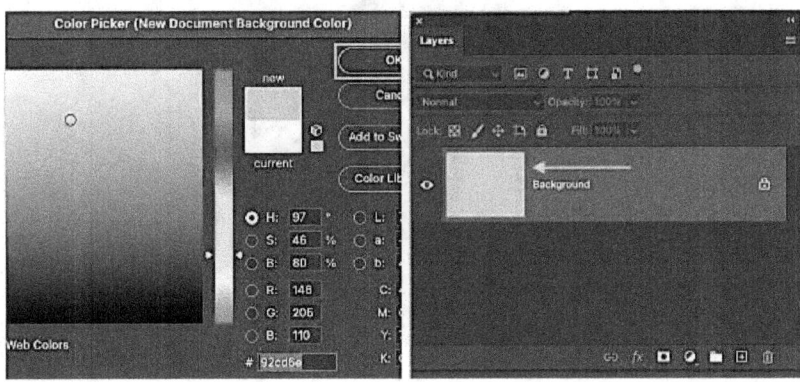

Adjusting the Background Color in an Existing Project

If you already have a project in progress, the background layer color is already determined.

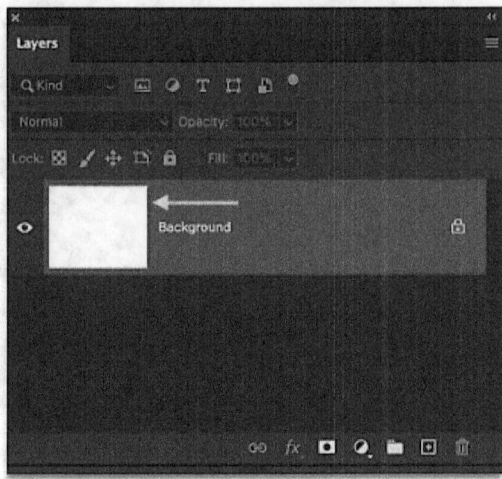

Fortunately, changing it is straightforward using a keyboard shortcut. Start by clicking on your foreground color at the bottom of your toolbar and choose a new color to fill your background layer.

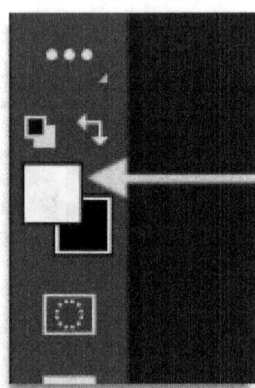

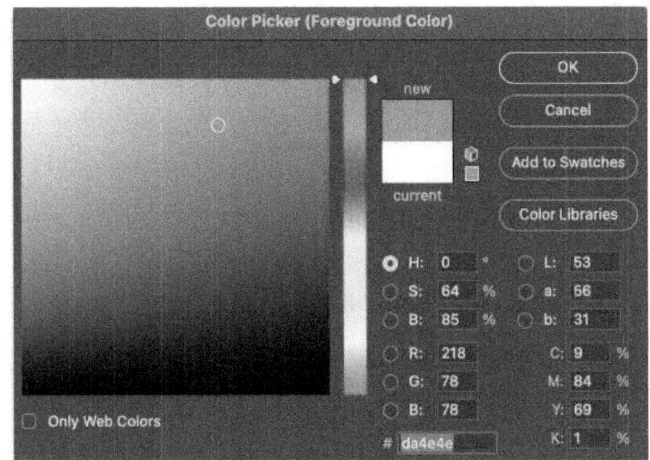

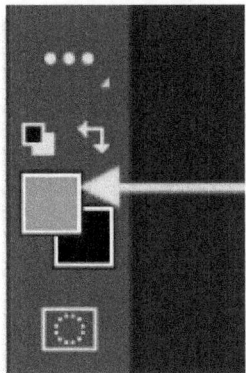

Once your foreground color is set, make sure your background layer is highlighted in the Layers Panel. To apply the new color, press Alt + Delete (PC) or Option + Delete (Mac) to fill the layer with your foreground color. This action works even if the layer is locked, instantly updating the background color.

Wishing to alter your background layer color in the future, you can repeat these steps at any time.

CHAPTER SIX

THE USE OF LASSO TOOLS

This feature in Photoshop is a freehand selection tool. In the context of this tool, "freehand" implies that the user guides the selection border using a mouse or pen tablet by drawing. It proves advantageous for swiftly creating selections without the need to manage additional settings like anchor points or curves, as required with the Pen tool. Similar to using the Brush tool to draw a line, the Lasso tool is employed to draw a selection.

While the Lasso tool provides a commendable degree of control and speed, it does so at the expense of precision. Selections made with the Lasso tool may require more refinement, especially when aiming for accuracy in intricate or detailed selections.

Nonetheless, mastering the Lasso tool is valuable, despite its occasional need for additional refinement. Each of its three tool variants comes with its own optimal use case. Let's delve into each variant, their settings, and the scenarios where they are most effective.

When to Employ the Lasso Tool in Photoshop

In most cases, the Lasso tool serves as an efficient choice for swift extractions, particularly when creating selections along uncomplicated, straight edges, or when precision is not a primary concern. It excels in scenarios involving images with rectangular or geometric shapes, such as buildings and picture frames.

Additionally, it proves ideal for rapidly eliminating sizable portions of an image that might be obstructive or deemed surplus, akin to tearing a piece of paper for quick removal.

How To Use Default Lasso

The keyboard shortcut for the Lasso tool is **L**, and it can be accessed from the Toolbar where its icon resembles a simple lasso rope. It is typically set as the default tool; however, if not, you can switch tools by right-clicking the icon and selecting the Lasso tool.

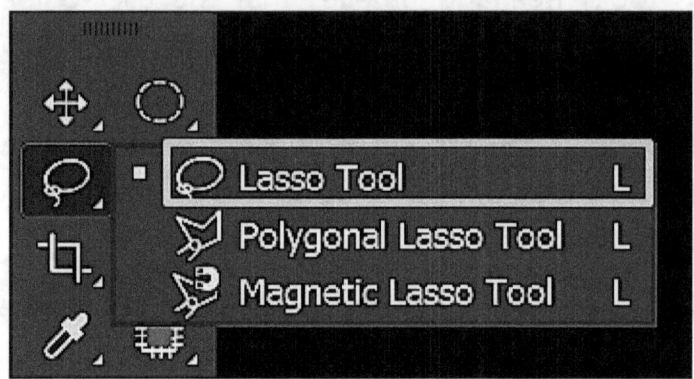

Before initiating your selection, ensure that the settings in the upper Settings bar are accurate. Focus on the Feather setting, where a Feather of 0px results in a sharp and crisp selection, while a higher Feather setting generates a softer edge. The pixel value determines the extent of softness in the edge. If the edge becomes excessively soft to the point of not selecting any pixels, a warning prompt will appear, prompting you to lower the Feather amount. For a slightly less sharp edge, enhancing extraction quality, consider setting the Feather to 1 – 5px.

Note that the Feather amount must be set before commencing the selection, and the selection path won't visually display the Feather amount. It is advisable to conduct a smaller test selection if planning to create a larger selection with Feather.

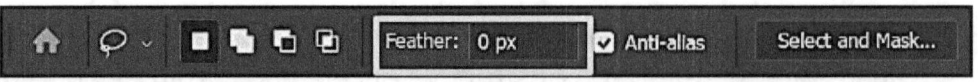

To make a selection, click and drag to draw a freehand selection path while holding down the mouse button.

To close the selection, either loop back to the starting point or release the mouse button, automatically closing the selection with a straight path leading to the starting point.

After creating a selection, add a Layer Mask to the desired layer for extraction. The Layer Mask will conform to the shape of the selection. In cases where quick selections without demanding precision are required, the default Lasso tool proves to be highly effective.

In the provided image, the Lasso tool is used to create a selection and add a layer mask to merge the drops from a layer set to Screen with the hand layer.

One of the primary advantages of the default tool is its effectiveness in making swift selections that don't demand precision.

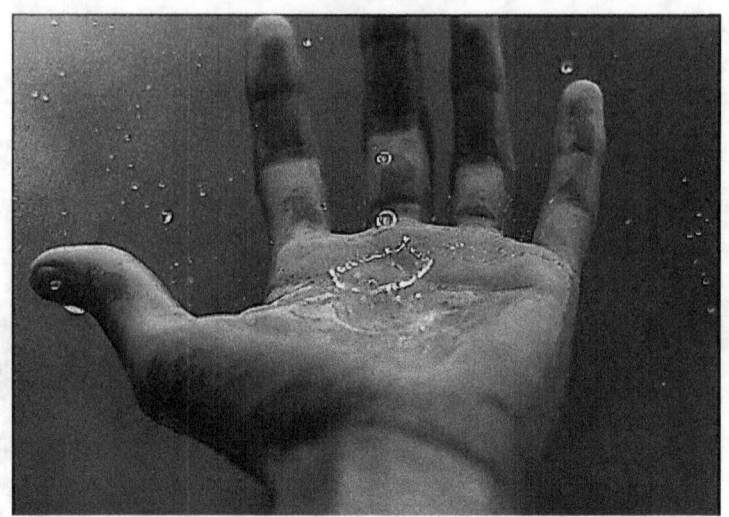

How to Effectively Utilize the Polygonal Lasso Tool

The Polygonal Lasso tool proves to be a valuable asset when precision is crucial for creating selections with straight edges or when extracting objects featuring hard angles. To access the Polygonal Lasso tool, either right-click the Lasso tool to open the fly-out menu or **press Shift + L** to cycle through different tools until you reach the Polygonal Lasso.

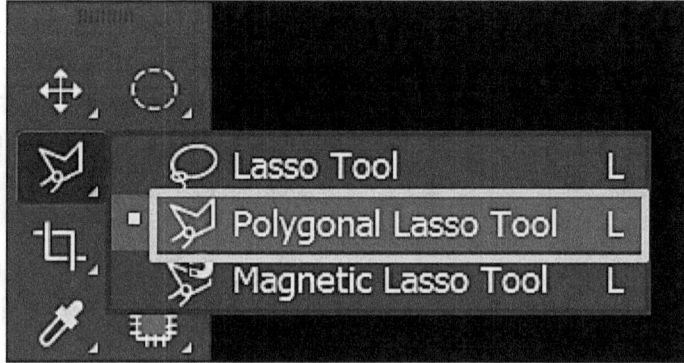

Similar to the default Lasso tool, the Polygonal Lasso tool includes a Feather setting. The Feather determines the softness of the selection edge, with a higher Feather resulting in a softer edge. A Feather setting of 0px ensures a completely sharp edge.

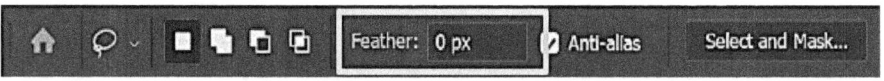

To initiate your selection, click on the image to set a starting point.

Subsequently, position the pointer at the desired endpoint for the first straight segment and click again. Each click generates an anchor point, guiding your path along straight and angled lines.

Conclude your path by clicking on the initial anchor point. In the example provided, I utilized the Polygonal Lasso tool to create a selection of the interior of a frame.

Following the selection, you can incorporate a mask into the image. The mask aligns with the shape of the selection, appearing exclusively within the frame.

Another quick method involves using **Ctrl+A (Windows) / Command+A (Mac)** to swiftly select the entire image. Subsequently, use Ctrl+C (Windows) / Command+C (Mac) to copy it to the clipboard. To integrate the image into the billboard, switch back to the original photo, navigate to the Edit menu at the top of the screen, and opt for the Paste Into command.

This tool is particularly effective for extracting elements such as modern buildings and signs, where precise straight lines and angles are essential.

Utilizing the Magnetic Lasso Tool for Precise Selections

When working in Photoshop, an array of selection tools is at your disposal, each designed for specific needs. The Magnetic Lasso Tool stands out by automatically adhering to the edges of high-contrast objects in an image, simplifying the process of selecting intricate details. In this tutorial, we delve into the steps of using the Magnetic Lasso Tool to select a specific object and refine its edges.

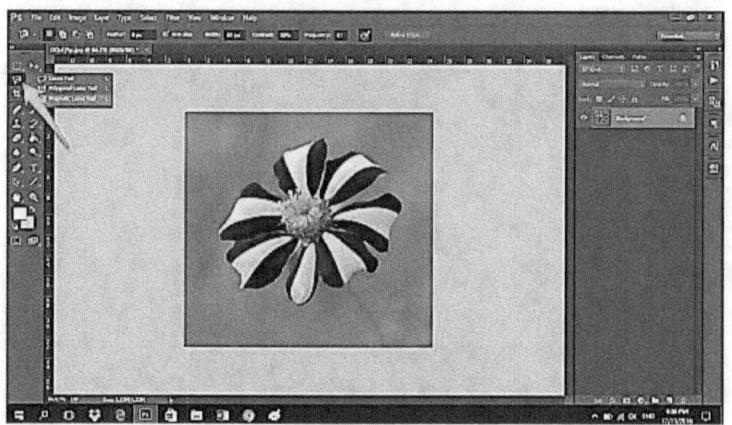

Accessing the Tool Commence by opening an image, such as a flower sourced from the internet. Locate the Magnetic Lasso Tool in the toolbox and select it to initiate the selection process.

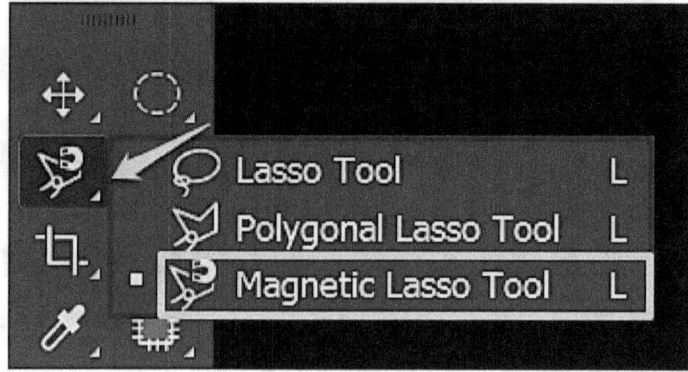

Click on a point in the image to establish the initial anchor point. Begin drawing with the Magnetic Lasso to outline the object you wish to select. The tool automatically generates anchor points, adhering to the edges of the object for a swift and precise selection.

To complete the selection, find the first anchor point to close the contour manually. Alternatively, expedite the process by double-clicking or pressing Enter at any point.

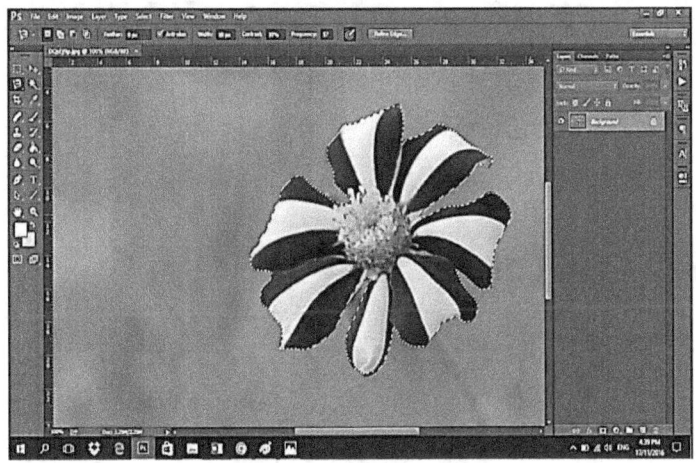

Before moving or duplicating the selection, enhance its quality by utilizing the Refine Edge feature. Right-click within the selection and choose "Refine Edge" to access tools for achieving smooth and polished edges.

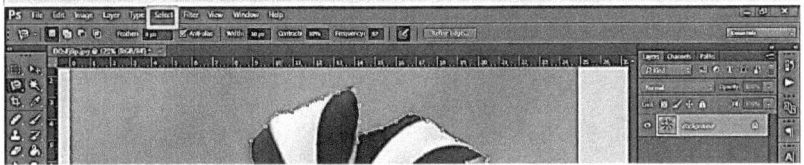

Duplicating or Moving the Selection Conclude the process by duplicating or relocating the refined selection. Press Ctrl + J to duplicate the selection, creating a new layer with the copied area. Alternatively, drag the selection to another document for seamless integration.

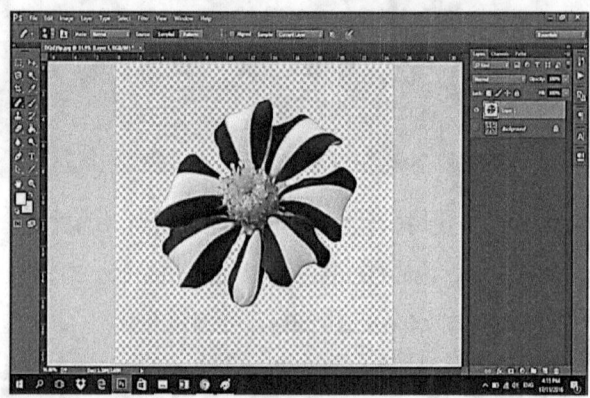

Mastering the Magnetic Lasso Tool and refining edges ensures meticulous selections, making it an indispensable technique for precise image manipulation in Photoshop.

USING THE MAGIC WAND TOOL

- Initiate the selection process by opting for the Magic Wand tool from the toolbar. Ensure that the layer you intend to select is active to focus your adjustments accurately.

- Position the cursor where you desire the selection, and with a simple click, watch as a new selection automatically materializes, encompassing the targeted area.

- Enhance the precision of your selection by employing various editing techniques. For instance, eliminate undesired areas from the selection by clicking on the "Subtract from the Selection" icon located in the Options bar. Alternatively, explore the versatile Quick

Mask mode in the sidebar, where you can refine your selection using tools such as the Eraser tool.

- In case your initial selection requires adjustments, exercise the flexibility to modify it. Deselect by using the keyboard shortcut Command+D on Mac or Ctrl+D on PC, providing you with the opportunity to recalibrate your selection according to your specifications.

- Experiment with the dynamic capability to invert your selection, thereby altering what is currently chosen. Facilitate this reversal by navigating to "Select › Inverse." This action transforms your selection, making it an invaluable feature for manipulating your chosen elements in a nuanced manner.

THE USE OF ERASER TOOLS

These tools are considered destructive, implying that the alterations they apply will be permanently integrated into your work unless the "undo" function is promptly employed.

Once the modifications are committed to your file, the changes made with the eraser tools become irreversible. To mitigate the risk of permanent alterations, it is advisable to operate on a duplicate layer when utilizing these tools.

Guide to Employing the Magic Eraser Tool in Photoshop

Locating the Magic Eraser tool is a straightforward process. Simply click and hold the eraser icon, then select the Magic Eraser Tool from the options.

At the top of the interface, take note of the settings panel. Adjust the Tolerance to suit your requirements. Ensure that both Anti-Alias and Contiguous options are selected, and set the Opacity to 100% for optimal results.

I will illustrate the process using the image below.

By setting the Tolerance to 32, a simple click on the area I wish to erase will prompt the system to select and erase pixels with colors similar to the clicked area, extending to adjacent regions.

As evident, the brush exhibited excessive tolerance, erasing portions of the flower's darker areas. After undoing this action with Control + Z (Win) or Command + Z (Mac), let's observe the impact of reducing the Tolerance to 10.

With this adjustment, only the darkest areas have been erased, yielding a more precise and accurate result like the one above.

Erase with the Eraser Tool

Locate the Eraser Tool by navigating to the eraser icon situated in the toolbar on the left.

If a different eraser tool is currently active, click and hold the icon, then select the Eraser Tool.

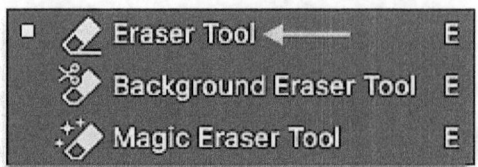

Functioning akin to a brush, this tool allows you to adjust parameters such as size, opacity, smoothing, and flow. You can seamlessly switch between brush, pencil, and block modes.

The eraser tool operates by eliminating the pixels you brush over. Unless recently used, the color is automatically set to white, giving the appearance of painting with a brush as you erase pixels. The erasure is permanent, and retrieval is only possible through the Undo function.

While the eraser tool is straightforward and convenient, it may lead to errors when tackling intricate areas. It is most effective for erasing simpler regions. Although it's technically possible to erase complex, jagged areas with this tool, it often demands significant time and effort. In such cases, opting for one of the other eraser brush tools is generally more efficient.

Alter Pixels with The Magic Eraser Tool

When utilizing the Magic Eraser tool on a layer, a click will transform all analogous pixels to transparency. In the case of a layer with locked transparency, the pixels are converted to the background color if clicked. Clicking on the background converts it to a layer, and all akin pixels become transparent.

You have the option to erase solely contiguous pixels or all akin pixels within the current layer.

1. Select the Magic Eraser tool.

2. In the options bar, perform the following:

- Set a tolerance value to determine the range of colors eligible for erasure. A low tolerance removes pixels with color values closely resembling the clicked pixel, while a high tolerance broadens the range of colors subject to erasure.

- Opt for Anti-aliased to smoothen the edges of the erased area.

- Choose Contiguous to erase only pixels contiguous to the clicked one, or deselect to erase all similar pixels in the image.

- Enable Sample All Layers to sample the erased color using combined data from all visible layers.

- Specify an opacity to define the strength of the erasure. An opacity of 100% eradicates pixels entirely, while a lower opacity erases pixels partially.

3. Click on the part of the layer you wish to erase.

Auto Erase with The Pencil Tool

Enable the Auto Erase feature for the Pencil tool to effortlessly paint the background color over regions with the foreground color.

Follow these steps:

1. Set the foreground and background colors.

2. Choose the Pencil tool.

3. Activate Auto Erase in the options bar.

4. Drag over the image.

When initiating the drag, if the cursor's center is positioned over the foreground color, the area is erased to the background color.

Conversely, if the cursor's center is over a region devoid of the foreground color, the area is painted with the foreground color.

UTILIZING WHITE BALANCE IN PHOTOSHOP

White balance in Photoshop refers to the adjustment of colors in an image to ensure that white appears truly white, without any unwanted color casts. When an image is taken, the color temperature of the light source can influence the colors in the photo. White balance correction helps neutralize these color shifts and produce more accurate and natural-looking colors.

In photography, different light sources (such as daylight, tungsten, fluorescent, etc.) have varying color temperatures. If the camera's white balance settings are not appropriately configured, the resulting image may appear too warm (yellow or orange) or too cool (blue). Correcting the white balance is crucial for achieving realistic and visually pleasing colors in your photographs.

Photoshop provides several tools for adjusting white balance, including the Color Balance, Levels, and Curves adjustments. These tools allow you to fine-tune the color balance in different tonal ranges of the image, correcting any color biases and ensuring that whites appear neutral.

Adjusting the white balance in Photoshop is a straightforward process that can significantly enhance the overall color accuracy of your images. Follow these steps to rectify white balance issues:

- Open your image in Photoshop.

- Navigate to the "Image" menu and select "Adjustments."

- Choose the "Color Balance" option.

- In the Color Balance dialog box, adjust the sliders for Shadows, Midtones, and Highlights until you achieve the desired color balance. Typically, you'll want to balance the warmth of the image by adjusting the levels of cyan and red, magenta and green, and yellow and blue.

- Optionally, you can use the "Auto Levels" feature by selecting "Auto" in the Color Balance dialog box. Photoshop will attempt to automatically adjust the color balance based on its algorithms.

- Another way to fix white balance is by using the "Levels" adjustment. Go to "Image" > "Adjustments" > "Levels." In the Levels dialog box, use the dropper tool to click on a neutral gray area in the image. Photoshop will automatically adjust the color balance based on the selected gray point.

- If you prefer a more manual approach, you can use the "Curves" adjustment. Go to "Image" > "Adjustments" > "Curves." In the Curves dialog box, adjust the individual color channels (Red, Green, and Blue) to fine-tune the color balance.

- Once you're satisfied with the adjustments, click "OK" to apply the changes.

However, working with white balance can be implemented using two methods ways such as the camera Raw method or the Curves method, but in this case Curve method will be considered.

Adjusting White Balance Using the Curve Method

Although the primary purpose of the Curves tool in Photoshop is often seen as adjusting exposure and contrast, it can also be utilized for white balance and color correction.

1. Generate a New Adjustment Layer

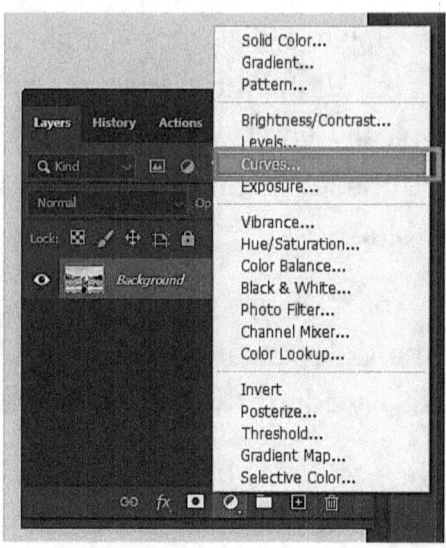

Choose Create New Adjustment Layer > Curves from the layer menu. Alternatively, you can utilize Photoshop keyboard shortcuts: Ctrl + M (for Windows) and Cmd + M (Mac).

2. Explore Pipette Options Photoshop white balance pipette options

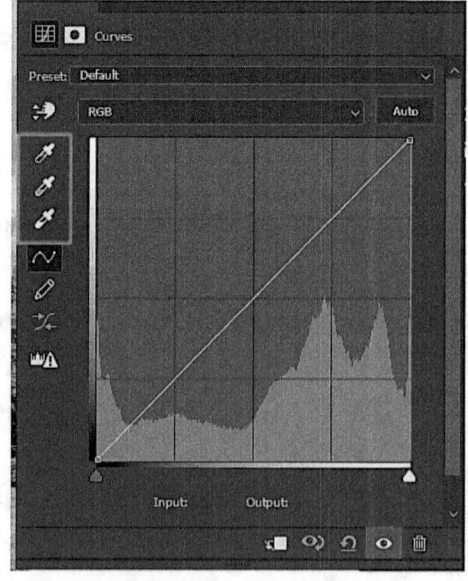

On the left side of the layer panel, you will find three droppers dedicated to white balance correction. Hovering over each dropper

provides pop-up hints guiding you on what to click and the subsequent steps.

3. Correct Areas in the Image The top dropper addresses the darkest areas, the middle one detects light shades, and the bottom one focuses on the lightest part of the image. If the colors change abruptly after clicking, you can click multiple times in the same area to achieve the desired result. Alternatively, explore various Photoshop actions, both free and paid, to enhance specific moods.

4. Evaluate the Outcome Review the result obtained with just three clicks. If satisfactory, the process is complete.

However, in the case of a portrait where skin tones may appear unrealistic, consider utilizing Photoshop portrait tutorials available online or on Adobe's official site. These tutorials cover a wide range of topics, including compositing, digital painting, special effects, and graphic design. Presented in different formats such as step-by-step written guides, video demonstrations, and interactive projects, these tutorials cater to various learning preferences.

GUARDING WHITE BALANCE IN VARIOUS LIGHTING SITUATIONS

Adjust Your White Balance Settings In-Camera

Adobe Camera RAW is a valuable tool for importing RAW images into Photoshop and making essential corrections.

1. Duplicate the Background Start by duplicating the background of the image. Hold the layer and drag it to the square with a plus sign below the layer panel.

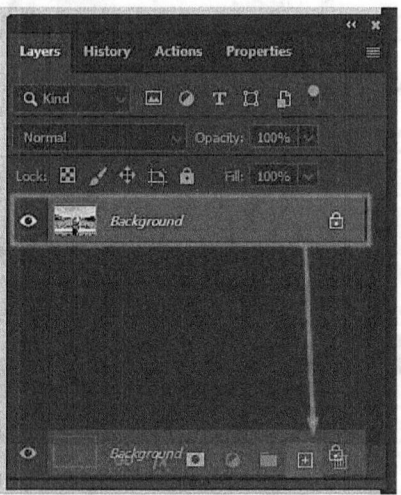

2. Convert to Smart Object Right-click on the layer and choose "Convert to Smart Object." This step is crucial for further editing.

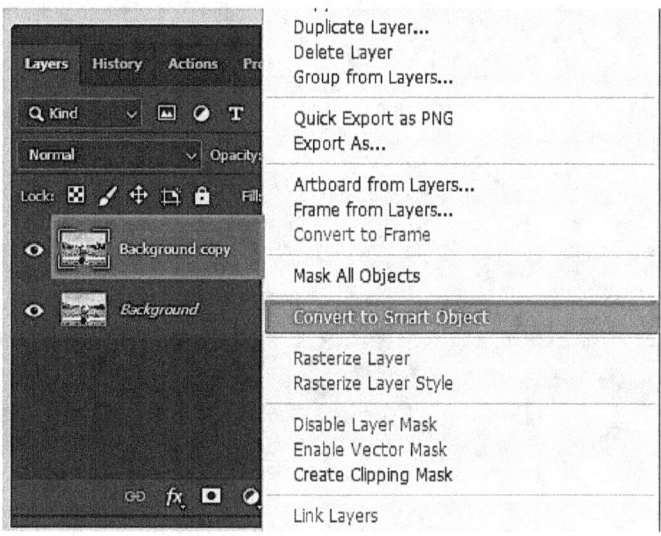

3. Select Camera Raw Filter Navigate to the Filter tab and choose the Camera Raw Filter option.

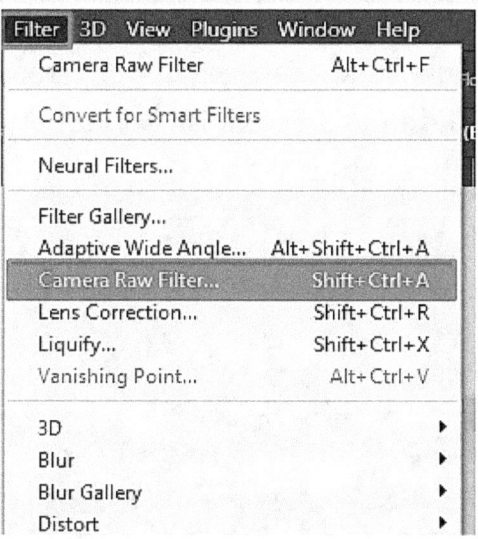

4. Choose a White Balance Mode In the White Balance panel, select a suitable mode for further editing. If you captured the photo and have a source code, press "As Shot" to preserve the color balance in Photoshop along with other picture settings. Auto mode may also yield satisfactory results.

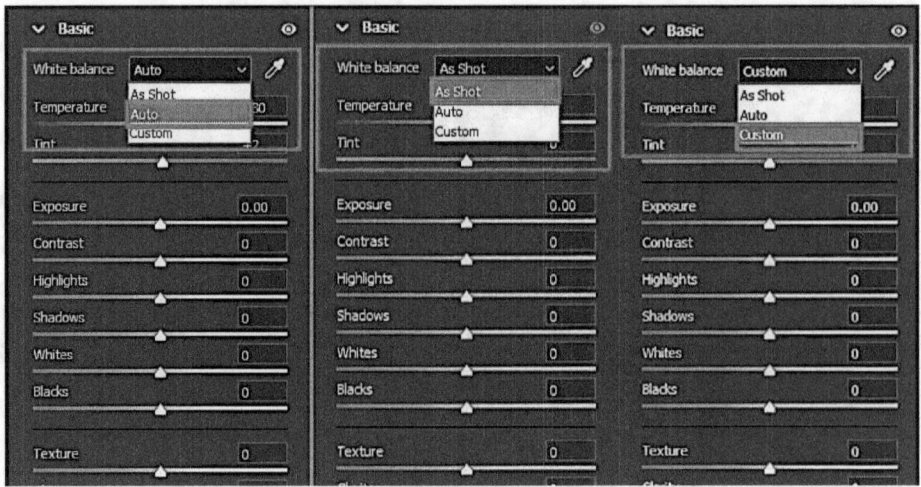

If needed, set the white balance manually using the Custom mode, adjusting the Temperature and Tint sliders responsible for WB.

5. Adjust the Desired Tone Evaluate the image and adjust as needed. If the whites appear cool, add warm tones using the Temperature and Tint sliders on the right-side menu. For portraits, address any reddish skin tones by introducing greenish shades with another slider.

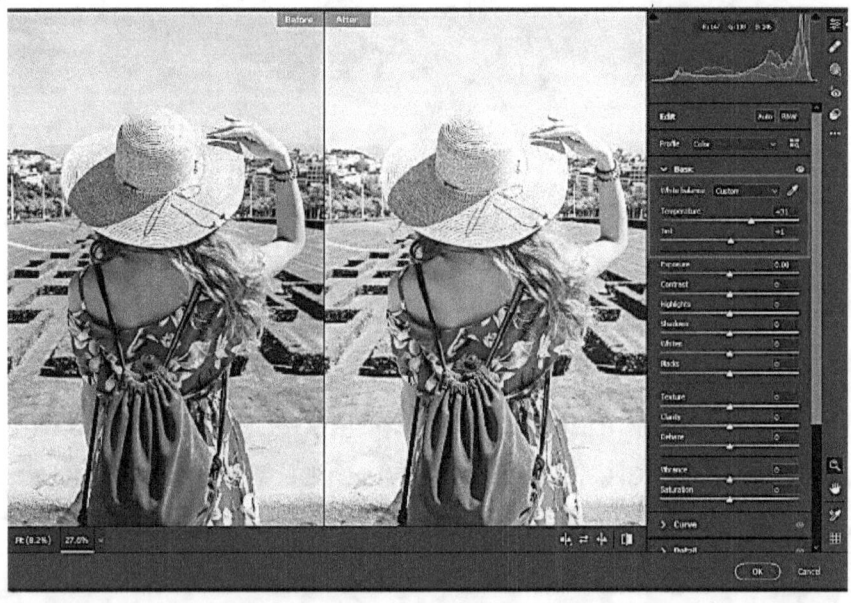

6. Utilize Camera Raw Filter for Final Edits If the result is not as expected, double-click on the Camera Raw indicator to reopen the window with the last settings, allowing you to make further adjustments.

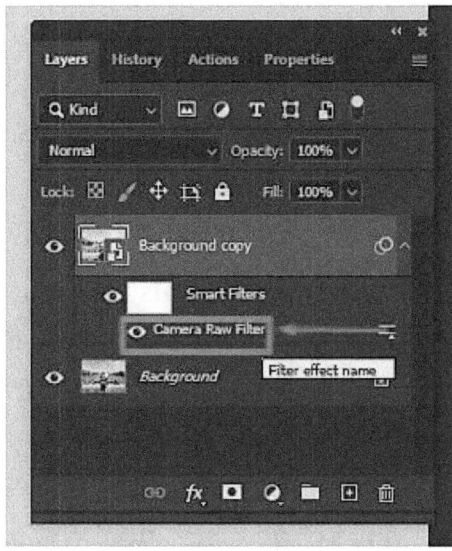

LEARNING ABOUT COLOR TEMPERATURES

Tungsten and daylight settings serve as the most commonly used white balance values, yet certain scenarios demand a more nuanced approach. Sets with mixed light sources often require relying on visual judgment rather than rigid rules. For instance, in an indoor scene illuminated by both artificial and natural light through a window, color temperatures can vary across the frame.

In such cases, it's crucial to identify the dominant light source and balance accordingly. If both sources are relatively equal, find a middle ground. Understanding the rules is essential to breaking them. Cinematographer Leonard compares cinematography to cooking, emphasizing the importance of knowing the recipe while letting personal taste be the final arbiter. Familiarize yourself with numbers, settings, and tools like scopes, but trust your eye to determine whether the image looks right, ensuring your monitors are accurately calibrated.

Videographer Hiroshi Hara recommends manually selecting white balance, typically starting with either tungsten or daylight balance and adjusting based on the specific situation. Building your set around a consistent color temperature prevents conflicting white balances. Hara emphasizes the importance of capturing the shot correctly in camera to minimize post-production manipulations.

While the human eye naturally adapts to various lighting conditions, cameras lack this automatic adjustment. It becomes necessary to instruct your camera on how to balance light, as otherwise, your frames may exhibit a magenta or bluish tint. Many digital cameras come equipped with presets for daylight and tungsten settings, yet you also have the option to manually set the white balance. When white-balancing an image, the goal is to introduce orange to counteract blue light or add blue light to counter orange light until the whites in the image achieve a true white appearance.

Daylight white balance.

designated configuration for capturing outdoor scenes illuminated by natural light. This specific choice is rooted in the characteristic cool and blue tones that outdoor light tends to exhibit. To ensure accurate color representation, particularly when dealing with elements like a white piece of paper, it is advisable to set the white balance to 5,600 K in outdoor environments. Natural light, being dynamic and diverse, offers a considerable range of temperatures, allowing for nuanced variations in color temperature. For instance, during the warm and golden hues of sunset, commonly referred to as the golden hour, the color temperature tends to be on the lower end of the Kelvin scale. Conversely, overcast days contribute to higher temperatures, resulting in cooler and bluer tones prevalent in such weather conditions. Understanding and adjusting for these variations play a crucial role in achieving accurate and visually appealing representations of outdoor scenes.

The Tungsten White Balance

The tungsten white balance setting is configured at 3,200 Kelvin (K) and is specifically tailored for indoor lighting scenarios. It's important to note that not all forms of artificial lighting precisely align with the 3,200 K temperature. Candlelight, for instance, tends to reside at the lowest and reddest segments of the color spectrum. Incandescent bulbs, ranging from soft white to warm white, typically occupy the mid-range range. On the other hand, the cool white illumination emitted by fluorescent lamps and LED lighting tends to lean towards the bluer end of the spectrum. This variability underscores the importance of selecting the appropriate tungsten white balance setting based on the specific artificial lighting conditions encountered in indoor environments.

COLOR PRODUCTION DURING POST-PRODUCTION EDITING

The choices you make during the shooting phase play a pivotal role in post-production, impacting the subsequent color grading process. This phase encompasses two essential aspects: color correction and color grading.

Color correction

Color correction entails the systematic restoration of accurate white balance, exposure, and contrast within an image. This method is fundamentally scientific, involving the analysis of graphs to ascertain appropriate exposure levels, black-and-white values, and the white balance of an image. Leonard emphasizes the importance of establishing a color temperature that aligns the whites, serving as a robust foundation for transitioning seamlessly into the creative aspects of the process.

Auto Color in Premiere Pro provides a quick and efficient way to correct color in video clips. Here's a step-by-step guide on how to use Auto Color:

1. Open the Lumetri Color panel by navigating to Window › Lumetri Color.

2. Place your play head on the specific clip you intend to color-correct within the timeline.

3. Under Basic Corrections in the Lumetri Color panel, locate and click the Auto button.

4. Fine-tune the intensity of the color correction using the Intensity slider. Additionally, for more precise adjustments, you can

individually refine each parameter by using the sliders available under Basic Corrections.

Color Grading

Color grading serves as the creative counterpart to the technical aspects of color correction. Once you've achieved balanced values through correction, you gain the ability to make subjective decisions that influence the color of light to suit your artistic preferences. In addition to adjusting temperature, you have the opportunity to fine-tune chromaticity, encompassing hue, and saturation, to create a stylized aesthetic or evoke a particular mood.

Leonard explains, "Maybe you want a scene to feel warmer because it's an emotional moment, or you aim to match the orange glow of golden hour. In these instances, you might adjust your color temperature to introduce warmer hues."

Different color temperatures are associated with distinct moods and atmospheres. For filmmakers, understanding the aesthetic impact of various lighting choices is crucial for conveying the desired visual narrative. For instance, fluorescent lights and bright white CFL (compact fluorescent lamp) or halogen bulbs are well-suited for sterile, professional settings, thanks to their cooler color temperatures. Conversely, light sources with warm tones, such as fire, incandescent bulbs, or the glow of a sunset, evoke feelings of nostalgia and warmth due to their lower Kelvin temperatures.

The Color Grading panel in Photoshop provides advanced controls for adding color to a grayscale image. Whether you want to apply a single color across the entire tonal range or create a split-tone effect with different colors for shadows, mid-tones, and highlights, the Color Grading panel allows for versatile and precise adjustments while keeping extreme shadows and highlights in black and white.

Here's a step-by-step guide

1. **Select an Image:** Choose a grayscale or black-and-white image as your starting point.

2. **Open Color Grading:** Click on "Edit" in the right panel, then open the "Color Grading" drop-down menu.

3. **Color Wheel Adjustments:** Use the color wheels provided for Shadows, Midtones, and Highlights to make color adjustments in your image. Each wheel allows you to choose a specific color for the corresponding tonal range. Dragging the points on the wheels adjusts the hue, while the inner circles control the saturation.

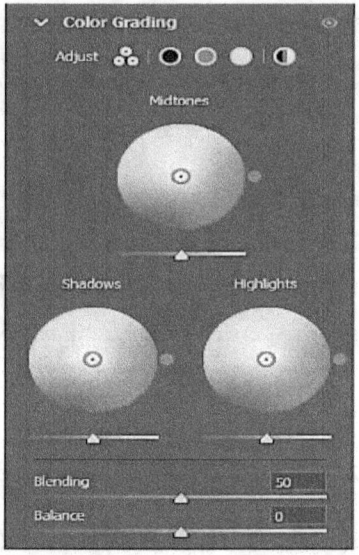

4. **Blending and Balance:** Adjust the "Blending" and "Balance" sliders to control the blending and balance of the color influences among Shadows, midtones, and Highlights. Positive values increase the influence of the Highlight controls, while negative values increase the influence of the Shadow controls.

5. **Additional Treatments:** Explore additional treatments available in the Color Grading panel, such as creating a cross-processed

look for a color image. Experiment with different settings to achieve the desired artistic effect.

This version of Photoshop allows you to have the flexibility to bring creative and nuanced color adjustments to grayscale or black-and-white images, allowing for sophisticated tonal enhancements and artistic expression.

CHAPTER SEVEN

GETTING STARTED WITH ADVANCED CUSTOM BRUSHES

Generate a brush tip from an image by employing any selection tool to choose the desired image area for your custom brush. The brush shape can have dimensions of up to 2500 pixels by 2500 pixels.

When painting, it's important to note that the hardness of sampled brushes cannot be adjusted. For a brush with sharp edges, set the **Feather to zero pixels.** Alternatively, for a brush with softer edges, increase the Feather setting.

Please be aware that if you opt for a color image, the brush tip image will be converted to grayscale. Additionally, any layer mask applied to the image will not impact the definition of the brush tip.

Proceed by selecting Edit > Define Brush Preset.

Provide a name for your brush and click **OK.**

CREATING A BRUSH AND SETTING PAINTING OPTIONS

1. Pick a painting, erasing, toning, or focus tool. Next, navigate to Window > Brush Settings.

2. In the Brush Settings panel, either opt for a brush tip shape or click on Brush Presets to select an existing preset.

3. Choose Brush Tip Shape on the left side and configure the necessary options.

4. For additional customization options, refer to the following topics:

- Incorporate dynamic elements into brushes

- Adjust scattering in a stroke

- Create textured brushes

- Define how a brush changes dynamically

- Utilize a graphics tablet for drawing or painting

5. To safeguard brush tip shape attributes (preserving them when selecting another brush preset), click the unlock icon. To reverse this, click the lock icon.

6. Save the brush for future use by selecting "New Brush Preset" from the Brush panel menu.

To permanently save or share your new brush, it must be part of a set of brushes. Opt for "Save Brushes" from the Brush Presets panel menu, and then save it to a new set or overwrite an existing set. If you reset or replace the brushes in the Brush Presets panel without saving them in a set, there is a risk of losing your newly created brush.

Bring In Brushes and Brush Collection

You have the flexibility to integrate a diverse range of both free and purchased brushes, such as those available in Kyle's Photoshop brush packs, into your Photoshop workspace. Here's a step-by-step guide:

1. In the Brushes panel, access the flyout menu and choose "Get More Brushes." Alternatively, right-click on a brush listed in the panel and opt for "Get More Brushes" from the contextual menu.

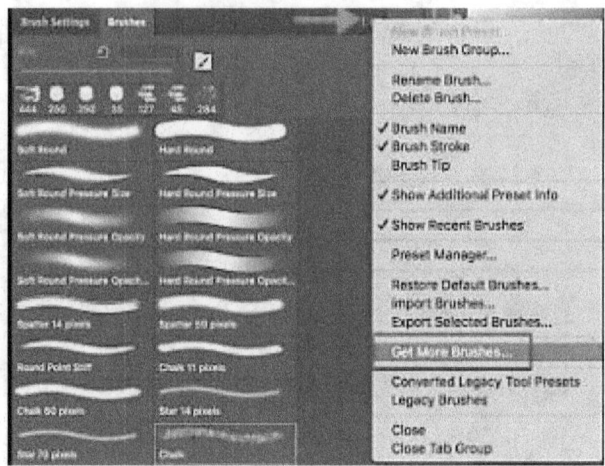

2. Download a desired brush pack, like Kyle's "Megapack."

3. With Photoshop open, double-click the downloaded ABR file.

4. The newly added brushes will now be visible in the Brushes panel.

An alternative method is to use the "Import Brushes" option in the Brushes panel flyout menu. Locate the downloaded ABR file and open it. This action will automatically include the downloaded brushes in the Brushes panel.

How to Generate a Colored Stamp Brush Using An Image

If you enjoy crafting posters, newsletters, or similar projects featuring a recurring graphic, you may want to transform it into a brush. Follow these step-by-step instructions to create a colored brush in Photoshop:

Launch Photoshop and initiate a new document

- Open Photoshop on your desktop and create a new document by choosing "File" > "New" from the menu (shortcut: Ctrl/Cmd N).

- In the new window, set the pixel size based on your desired brush dimensions, typically between 200 and 400 pixels.

- Scroll down to "Background Contents," choose "Transparent," and click OK to avoid a solid box around your brush.

Generate the brush content

- Paint, use shapes, or copy a selection from a photo to create the content of your brush.

- Ensure the background remains transparent.

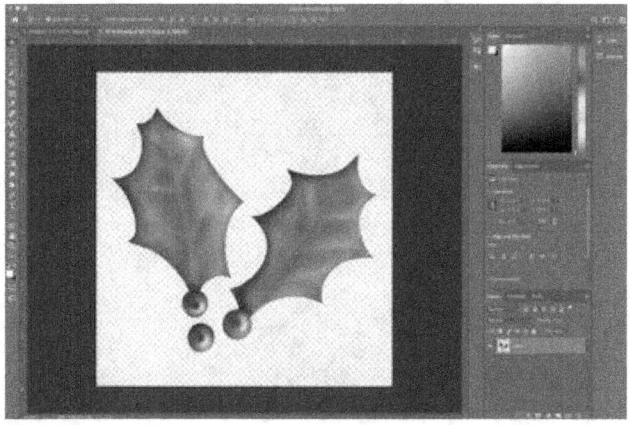

Select the Mixer Brush Tool

- Long-click on the brush tools to access the flyout and choose the Mixer Brush Tool.

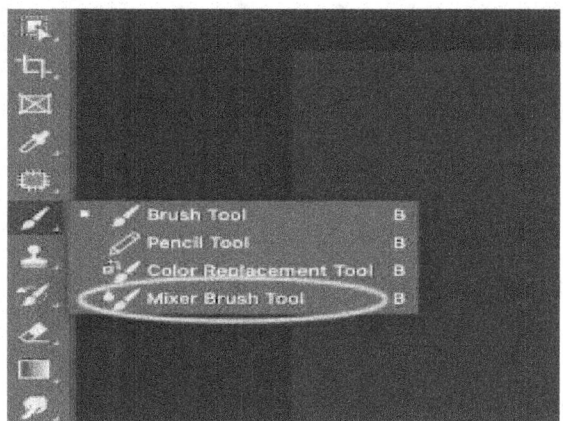

- Opt for the hard round default brush.

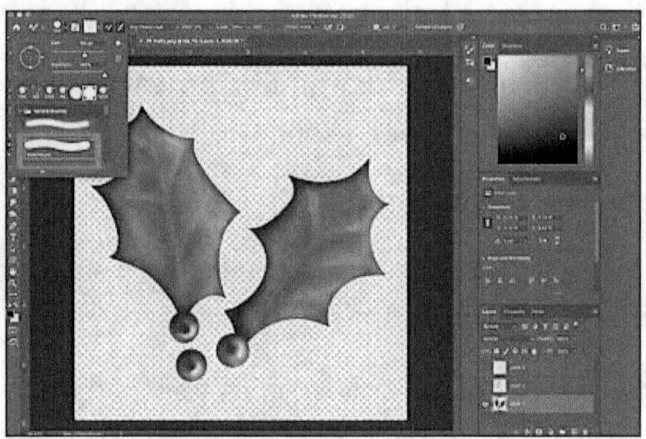

Configure the Mixer Brush Tool settings

- Set options to Dry, Heavy Load, Wet: 0%, Load 100%, and Flow 100%.

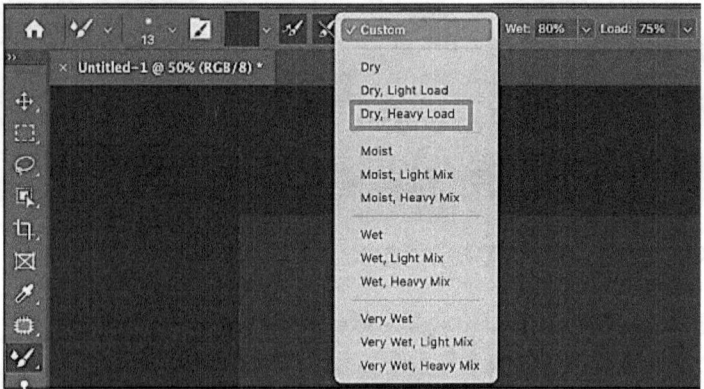

Capture the brush image

- Adjust the brush size to accommodate your image.

- Hold the Alt/Option key and click in the center of your image to capture the brush.

- The image will appear in the Current Brush Load swatch at the top.

Adjust the brush settings

- From the main menu, select Window > Brush Settings to open the brush options.

- Under Brush Tip Space, move the slider to space out the image.

- Click on Shape Dynamics and change the Angle Jitter Control option to Direction.

- Optionally, for pressure-sensitive pens, set the Size Jitter control to Pen Pressure.

- Close the Brush Settings panel.

Save and name your brush settings

- Click on the + symbol at the bottom right of the brush settings.

- Check "Include Color" and, if desired, "Capture Brush Size in Preset" and "Include Tool Settings."

- Name your brush and click OK to save it.

Use your new brush

- Create a new file or add a layer and try out your new brush.

- For a border, stamp the brush once, hold down the shift key, and stamp where you want the last one.

- A single click works as a stamp while brushing creates a series of stamps following your stroke with the set spacing.

Create A Brush And Set Painting Options

Choose a painting, erasing, toning, or focus tool, and then navigate to Window > Brush Settings.

Within the Brush Settings panel, opt for a brush tip shape or click on Brush Presets to select an existing preset.

Navigate to Brush Tip Shape on the left side and configure the desired options.

For additional customization of the brush, refer to the following topics:

- Integrate dynamic elements into brushes

- Adjust scattering in a stroke

- Develop textured brushes

- Define dynamic changes in a brush

If you're using a graphics tablet, explore drawing or painting techniques with it.

To lock the attributes of the brush tip shape (keeping them intact when selecting another brush preset), click the lock icon. To unlock the tip, click the unlock icon .

For future use, save the brush by selecting "New Brush Preset" from the Brush panel menu.

To permanently save or share your new brush, it must be part of a set. Choose "Save Brushes" from the Brush Presets panel menu, and then save it as a new set or overwrite an existing set. If you reset or replace the brushes in the Brush Presets panel without saving them in a set, there is a risk of losing your newly created brush.

CHAPTER EIGHT

GROUP IN PHOTOSHOP

Generating a cluttered and chaotic layers panel is effortless, particularly when layer groups in Photoshop are overlooked. Utilizing groups provides a straightforward method to organize your layer panel and maintain cohesion among related layers. This not only simplifies the process of editing multiple layers simultaneously but also enhances the efficiency of locating specific layers. In this tutorial, you will discover how to effortlessly group layers in Photoshop by employing convenient shortcuts to expedite the procedure.

However, if you prefer a manual approach, fear not; we will also cover how to accomplish everything without shortcuts. Let's embark on the journey

THE IMPORTANT OF GROUPING LAYERS IN PHOTOSHOP

Mastering the skill of creating groups in Photoshop is essential for maintaining organized and readily accessible layers related to your project. In portrait editing, for instance, it proves beneficial to group relevant adjustments such as hair, skin retouching, or color adjustments into distinct groups. This approach prevents a cluttered stack of layers, as grouping segments your layers and enhances the efficiency of your workflow.

Another advantage of grouping layers is the ability to apply the same adjustment to multiple photos simultaneously. When adjustments are made to a group, it impacts every layer within, significantly expediting the editing process by allowing you to implement a single adjustment across several layers simultaneously. No longer is there a need for individual adjustments when utilizing groups!

Additionally, creating groups facilitates the seamless movement of multiple layers as a unit. By selecting a group layer, you can relocate all its contents simultaneously. This feature is particularly handy if you wish to keep specific layers together on your canvas, such as text or clone stamp adjustments.

Once you've mastered the art of creating groups in Photoshop, your layer panel becomes more organized and easily navigable. Your layers can now be appropriately categorized and sorted based on their contents, simplifying the process of locating them. As an alternative to grouping layers, you also have the option to link layers together.

HOW TO ORGANIZE LAYERS IN PHOTOSHOP

Before forming a group, you must first choose the multiple layers you intend to group. Simply hold down Command (Mac) or Control (Win) and click on the desired layers to highlight them.

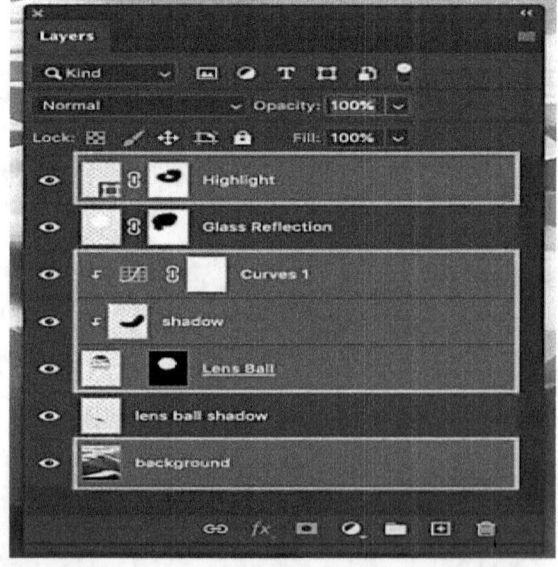

Now, there are two straightforward methods to create your group: a keyboard shortcut or clicking the group layer icon.

Keyboard Shortcut for Creating Groups

With your selected layers, press Command + G (Mac) or Control + G (PC) to instantly create a group. All the highlighted layers will be consolidated into a group folder.

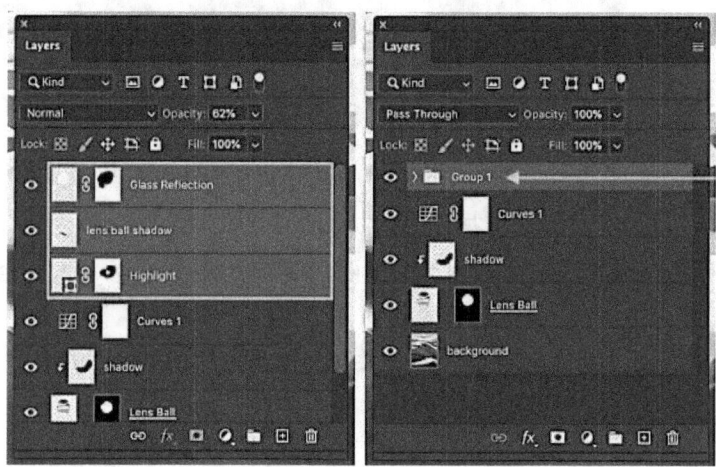

Creating Groups Manually

Once again, select the layers you want to include in your group. With the layers highlighted, click on the folder icon located at the bottom of the Layers panel.

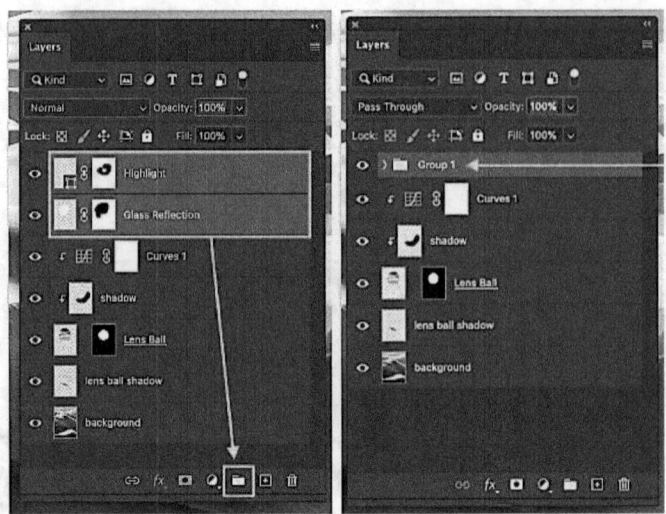

Both options are effective for anyone seeking to organize layers in Photoshop. While the keyboard shortcut offers a time-saving advantage, knowing the manual method is always beneficial!

DETERMINING IF A LAYER RESIDES WITHIN A GROUP

When dealing with numerous layers in your panel, discerning whether they are part of a group folder can be challenging. To clarify, there are two straightforward methods to confirm whether a layer is indeed inside a group.

The simplest approach involves hiding the contents of the group folder. Click on the arrow to the left of the folder icon. If the layer in question remains visible, it indicates that it is not part of the group.

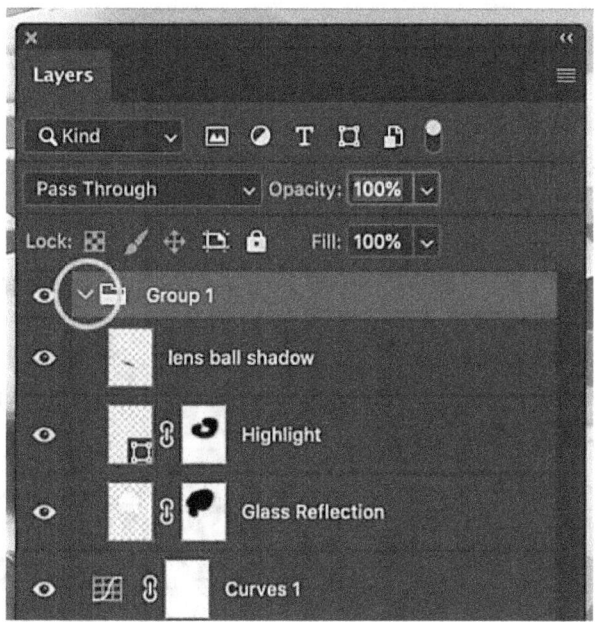

In such cases, effortlessly drag and drop the layer into the group until it becomes enveloped within the folder. You can retrieve it later when you reveal the group.

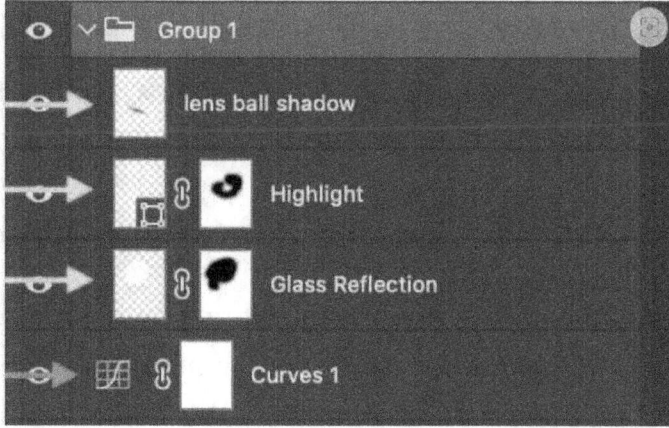

Alternatively, if your group layer is expanded, observe how its contents are indented in the layers panel. These indentations signify that the layer is within a group.

Removing a Layer from a Group

Creating a group in Photoshop doesn't lock you into a fixed arrangement. You can continuously edit its contents. To remove a layer from a group, click on the layer and drag it outside of the group. The layer will now exist independently in the Layers panel.

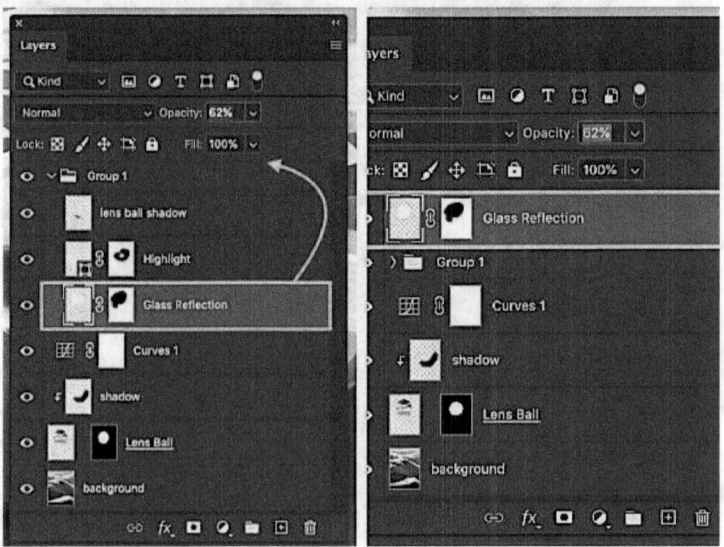

For removing multiple layers simultaneously, highlight the necessary layers and repeat the same steps.

Ungrouping All Layers in Photoshop

If you wish to dissolve a group entirely, a straightforward keyboard shortcut can ungroup all layers simultaneously. With the group layer selected, press Command + Shift + G (Mac) or Control + Shift + G (PC).

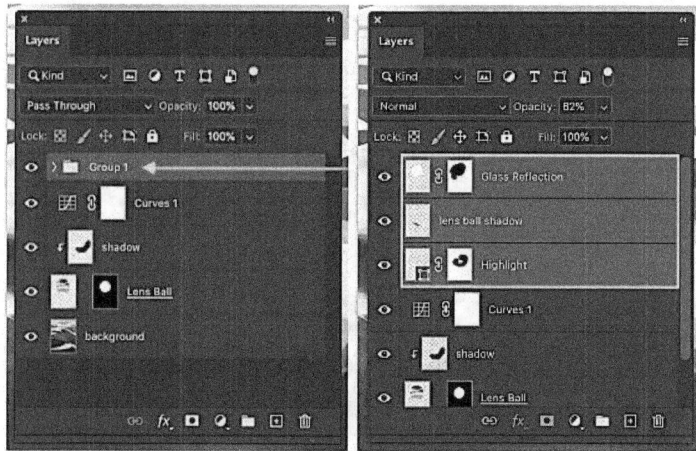

Alternatively, right-click on the group and choose 'ungroup layers.' The decision is yours!

How to Group Two Distinct Sets Together

For enhanced organization, consider incorporating groups within folders containing other groups.

Choose the group you wish to designate as the 'sub-group.'

Drag and drop it into the designated parent group.

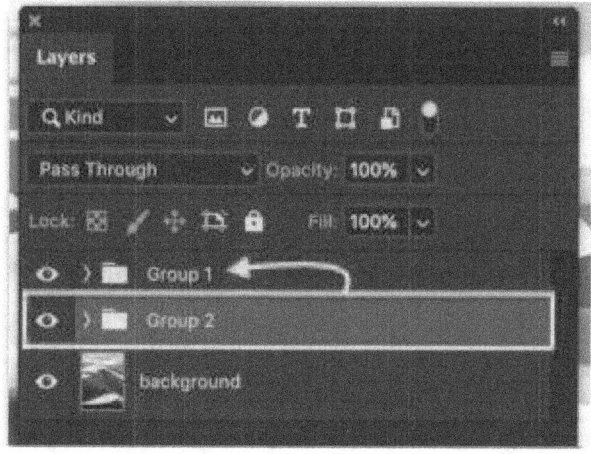

Both groups will now be located within the same overarching parent group.

CHAPTER NINE

THE PHOTO CORRECTION TOOLS THE RED EYE TOOL

The advanced functionality of the Red Eye Correction tool within our software empowers users with an effortless and efficient way to identify and eliminate the unwanted red-eye effect from their photographs. This intelligent tool is designed to automatically detect red eyes within the image, utilizing sophisticated algorithms that analyze the color distribution and characteristics of the eyes.

In the event that the automatic detection does not identify any instances of red eyes, users have the flexibility to take matters into their own hands by employing the manual marking feature. This enables a seamless transition between automated and user-controlled correction methods, ensuring that every user, regardless of their level of expertise, can achieve impeccable results.

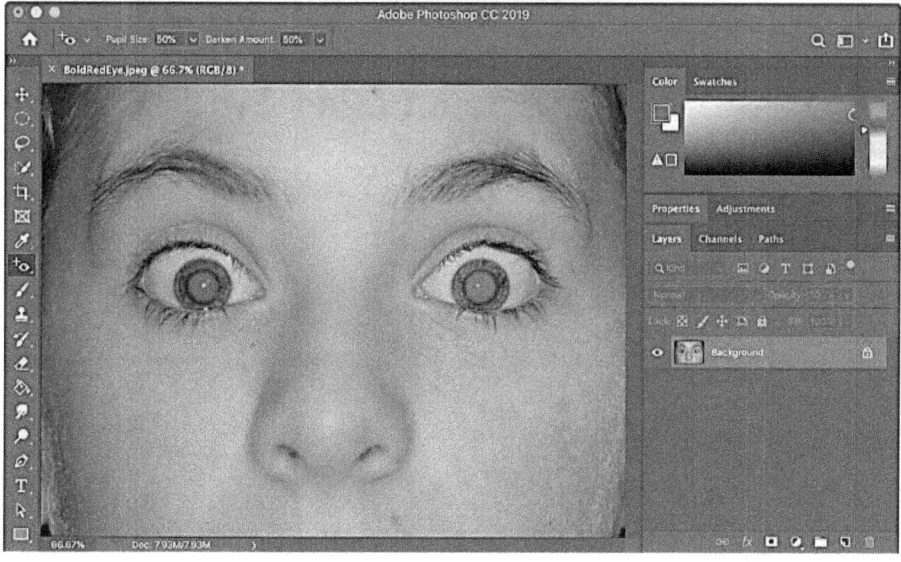

To manually mark red eyes, users can initiate the process by selecting the Red Eye Correction tool and navigating to the designated area on the image. With a simple click-and-drag motion, users can effortlessly guide the mouse cursor over the red eye region, allowing the tool to intelligently recognize the boundaries of the affected area. The result is a precise and defined circular marking encapsulating the red eye, providing a visual representation of the correction to be applied.

This hands-on approach not only grants users a sense of control and precision in the correction process but also serves as a valuable tool for refining the automated detection results. By allowing users to fine-tune the correction process through manual marking, our software ensures that the final output meets the user's expectations with unparalleled accuracy and attention to detail.

In essence, the Red Eye Correction tool combines the convenience of automatic detection with the precision of manual marking, offering a comprehensive solution to address the common issue of red-eye artifacts in photographs. This intuitive and versatile feature embodies our commitment to providing users with a powerful yet user-friendly toolset for enhancing the quality of their images.

Procedures for Removing Red-Eye in Photoshop

Removing red eyes from photos in Photoshop is a straightforward process. This tutorial will guide you through three simple steps to eliminate red-eye effects effortlessly.

1. Begin by opening your photo containing red-eye in Photoshop.

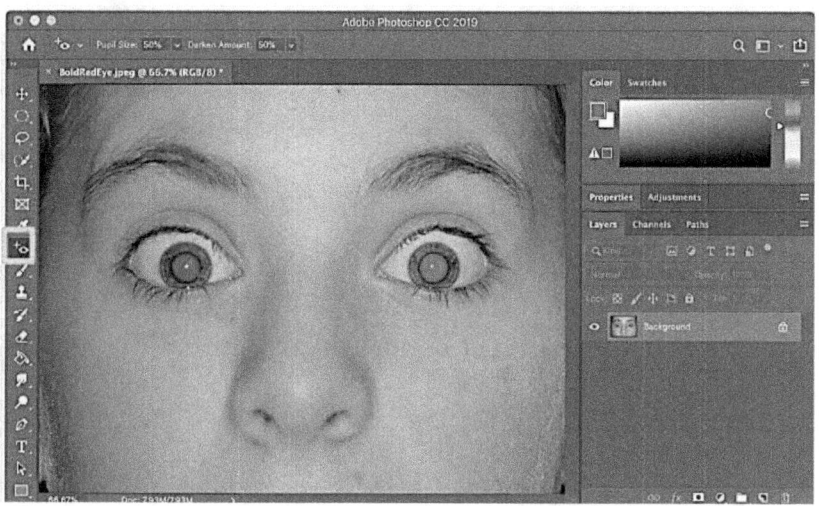

2. In the second step, select the Red Eye Tool.

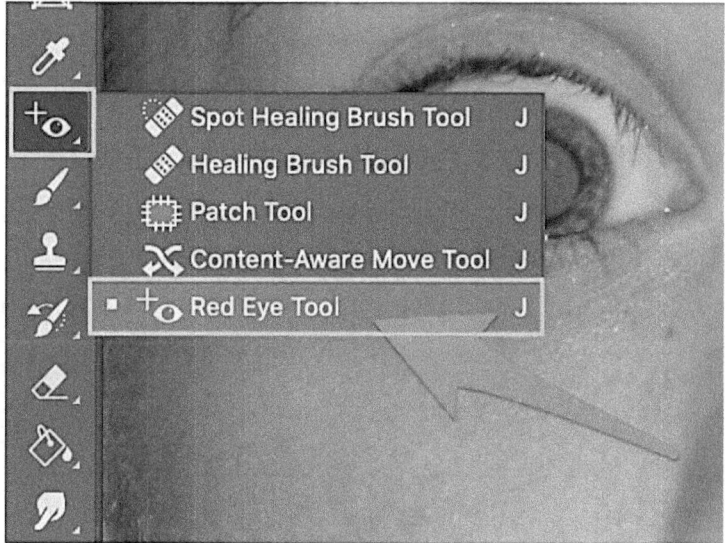

3. For the third step, click anywhere in the red part of each eye using the Red Eye Tool.

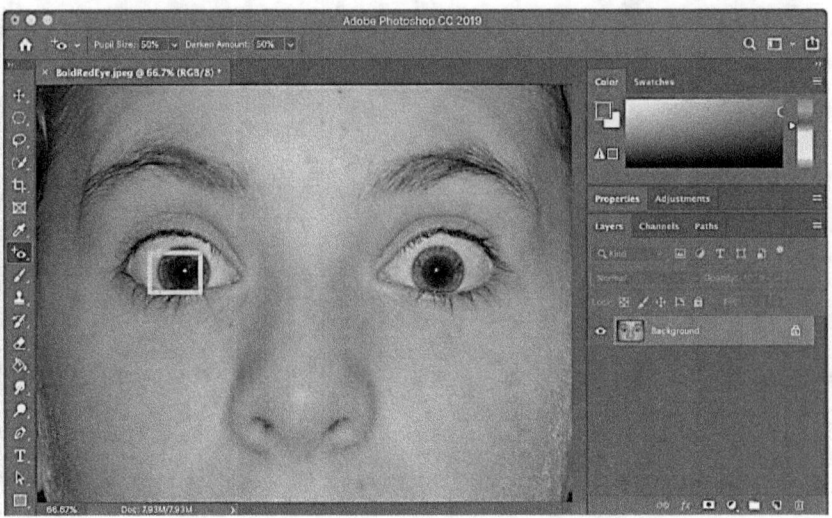

Congratulations! You've completed the red-eye removal process.

If the results aren't precisely what you're aiming for, consider the following adjustments:

- **Pupil Size and Darken Amount Settings:** You can fine-tune the results by adjusting the Pupil Size and Darken Amount settings. While these adjustments may not be necessary in most cases, they can be helpful in achieving the desired outcome.

The Pupil Size setting determines the area to darken, while the Darken Amount setting controls the intensity of the darkening effect.

Refer to image 174 for a visual guide.

- **Refinement Using Red Eye Tool:** If a single click doesn't completely address the red-eye issue, try clicking and dragging with the Red Eye Tool to encompass the entire red area. This technique can be useful if clicking on the red eye alone doesn't yield the desired results.

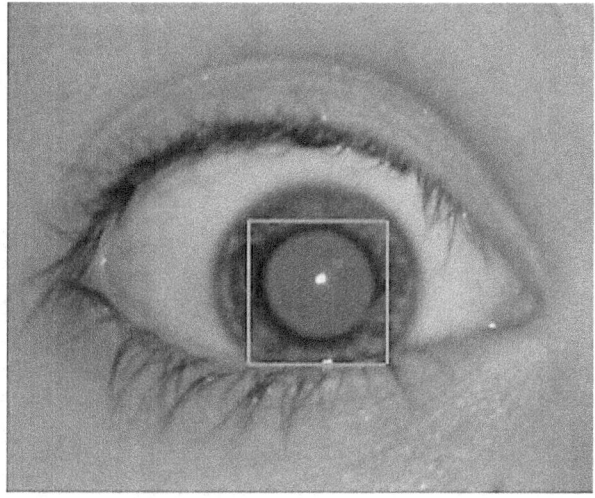

Remember, as each photo is unique, you might need to experiment with these settings to achieve the optimal look. Feel free to explore different areas of the red-eye and vary the sizes to find the most effective adjustments for your specific photo.

MASTERING THE PHOTOSHOP DODGE AND BURN TOOLS

In this tutorial, we will explore methods to enhance your outcomes while utilizing the Photoshop Dodge and Burn tools. Although these tools wield significant power, mastering them can prove challenging. To address this, I suggest an alternative approach to Dodging and Burning using Blending Modes.

Dodging and Burning is a valuable technique for infusing vitality and intrigue into your photographs. Even minor adjustments with the Photoshop Dodge and Burn tools can yield noteworthy enhancements. The results of my Dodging and Burning, combined with selective saturation increases, are visible below. The technique's potency lies in its ability to target specific areas of an image.

Before · After

The rationale behind employing Dodge and Burn

Dodging and Burning originated in the black-and-white darkroom, primarily employed to add interest to flat-looking images. In those times, black and white photos often lacked contrast, appearing lifeless in print. Dodging and Burning helped enhance these photos by making certain areas more pronounced and features more prominent.

When Dodging and Burning are applied selectively to areas of an image, they can either lighten or darken those areas. Our brains naturally direct attention towards lighter areas and away from darker ones when viewing a photo. This subconscious mechanism aids in directing viewers' attention. Additionally, differences in tone capture our attention, allowing us to perceive detail and depth. Selectively dodging and burning can add depth to photos, creating separation between subjects.

In traditional darkroom Dodging, exposure to an area was decreased, often achieved by placing an object between the light source and the photographic paper. This reduced exposure resulted in a lighter appearance in the final print. Conversely, Burning involves applying additional exposure to areas that might appear too light.

The Photoshop Dodge and Burn Tools

The Dodge and Burn Tools constitute a trio within the Photoshop Tools palette, with the Sponge Tool being the third member. While we won't delve into the details of the Sponge Tool here, it serves the purpose of selectively adjusting color saturation—either increasing or decreasing. To illustrate, consider the comparison between the initial and final images at the beginning of this article. The enhanced saturation of the foreground leaves on the path is achieved by first darkening them with the Dodge tool and subsequently intensifying their colors with the Sponge Tool.

Depending on your recent tool selection, any of the three tools (Dodge, Burn, and Sponge) may appear in the Tools Palette. By right-clicking on the current tool in the palette, a popup menu emerges, displaying the other tools within the group, and allowing you to make a selection.

Controlling the Dodge and Burn Tools

It's crucial to remember that both the Dodge and Burn tools in Photoshop are Brush Tools. The Burn Tool darkens areas, while the Dodge Tool lightens them. Upon selecting either tool, you'll find controls in the Context Sensitive toolbar at the top of the screen, as shown in the screenshot below.

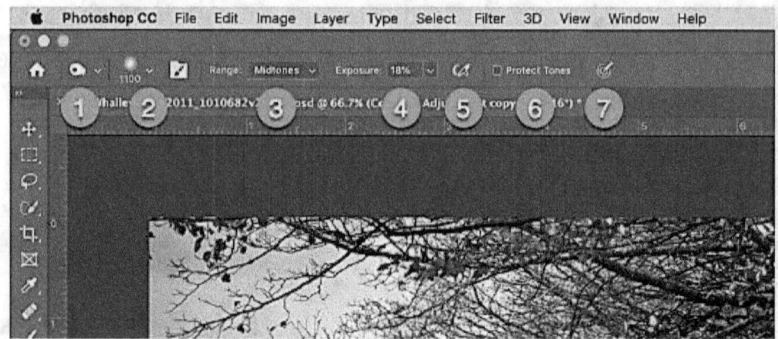

These tools share the same controls:

- Configuration options can be saved as a Tool Preset for future use.

- Adjustments to the brush's Size, Hardness, and other characteristics are made here.

- The Range dropdown targets the tonal range affected by the brush, including Highlights, Midtones, and Shadows.

- Exposure determines the strength of the effect, with higher values producing a more pronounced impact.

- The airbrush effect can be toggled on/off for a gradual buildup of adjustments.

- Protect Tones prevents changes in saturation while using the tools.

- Pressure controls are available for graphics tablet users with pressure-sensitive pens.

How to Use the Dodge and Burn Tools

To maximize the effectiveness of the Photoshop Dodge and Burn tools, begin by creating an editing plan. This involves sketching a line drawing of your photo and deciding which areas to lighten or darken, along with the choice of targeting highlights, shadows, or midtones. While this may seem time-consuming, it proves invaluable in understanding how to enhance your photo. Alternatively, you can achieve this by drawing on an empty layer within the image, as illustrated below.

1. Utilize Layers for Dodging and Burning For optimal results when using the Photoshop Dodge and Burn tools, it's advisable to apply them on a duplicated image layer. These tools are considered destructive as they directly impact the image pixels, making it challenging to readjust in subsequent editing sessions. Applying the tools on a separate layer provides better

control over the effect, allowing you to modify the layer's opacity and blending mode.

To create a new layer for Dodging and Burning, employ the keyboard shortcut Shift + Ctrl + Alt + E (Shift + Option + Command + E on a Mac). Pressing these keys simultaneously generates a "Stamp Layer," essentially a duplicate of all visible layers in the image condensed into a new layer. Ensure you click on a visible layer at the top of your Layers Window before using the keystrokes to ensure their effectiveness.

2. Avoid Default Settings The default strength of the Photoshop Dodge and Burn tools is excessively intense. Using them at their default strength may potentially compromise your results. A recommended starting exposure strength for the tools is between 3% and 5%. This allows you to gradually and naturally build up the Dodging and Burning effect.

In summary, resist the urge to rush the process.

3. Exercise Caution: It's easy to go overboard with the Photoshop Dodge and Burn tools, resulting in areas of your image becoming entirely black or white, depending on the tool in use. This can be visually unappealing and challenging to notice while you're in the midst of the editing process. The issue often becomes apparent only upon returning to the image later.

To check for potential loss of detail, consider adding a threshold layer to the top of your image layers in the Layers Window. Navigate to "Layers | New adjustment layer | Threshold..." in the menu. This action transforms your image into a black-and-white version.

Adjust the slider in the Properties window left and right. As you move the slider, the display reveals pixels lighter or darker than the set threshold. Check at values 8 and 249. At 8, look for large areas darker than this; if found, you may have darkened them excessively. At 249, look for extensive white areas. While not pure black and white, these values are dark and light enough to simulate that appearance on a screen or in a print.

After checking the threshold levels, deactivate the layer by clicking on the eye icon to the left of the layer in the Layers Window. Resume working on your image until you're ready to reevaluate.

The Use of Sponge Tool in Adobe Photoshop

In the context of enhancing the visual allure of a sunset image, a subtle touch of color manipulation can go a long way. In the depicted scenario, attention is drawn to the right side of the image, where a gentle hue between the clouds, attributed to the setting sun, beckons for amplification. The process begins with a strategic application of the Sponge Tool in Adobe Photoshop.

To initiate this transformation, a prudent approach involves duplicating the Background Layer, a move encapsulated by naming the duplicate layer as "Sponge." The rationale for opting not to duplicate the Dodge Layer is elucidated by the nuanced layering order. The Sponge layer, positioned beneath the Dodge layer, accommodates the masked tower, thereby preserving the hierarchical integrity of the editing process.

Selecting the Sponge Tool, the artist navigates the interface to the Saturate mode, setting the Flow value to a robust 100%. Armed with these configurations, the digital brush becomes a dynamic instrument for color enhancement. As the artist delicately paints over the designated area, the colors within that region gradually intensify in saturation. It's a methodical process that demands a keen eye for detail and an appreciation for the subtleties inherent in Photoshop manipulation.

Crucially, the philosophy underlying this Photoshop endeavor emphasizes subtlety over extravagance. The objective is not to orchestrate dramatic overhauls but rather to delicately accentuate specific elements within the image, allowing them to "pop" without overwhelming the visual narrative. This measured and contemplative approach to image enhancement encourages practitioners to invest time in scrutinizing the intricacies of the photograph, devising a thoughtful strategy, and executing adjustments with a deliberate and gradual hand. In this realm of digital artistry, restraint often yields more compelling and refined results, as the photographer harnesses the power of Photoshop to subtly elevate the visual impact of their composition.

THE SPOT-HEALING BRUSH TOOL

Understanding the Functionality of the Spot Healing Brush Tool:

As previously explained, the Spot Healing Brush tool serves the purpose of remedying blemished areas by leveraging the color, shading, luminosity, and texture of the surrounding regions as a reference.

To employ the Spot Healing Brush tool, a straightforward approach involves clicking directly on the targeted blemish. Upon doing so, the tool assesses the color, tone, shading, luminosity, and texture of the adjacent area, subsequently replicating these attributes onto the marked spot.

Let's illustrate the application of the Spot Healing Brush tool by addressing a mole in the nose area. By adjusting the brush size—accomplished by typing "[" to decrease and "]" to increase—we ensure the brush adequately covers the entire spot.

Once the Spot Healing Brush encompasses the targeted area, a simple click on the spot initiates the healing process.

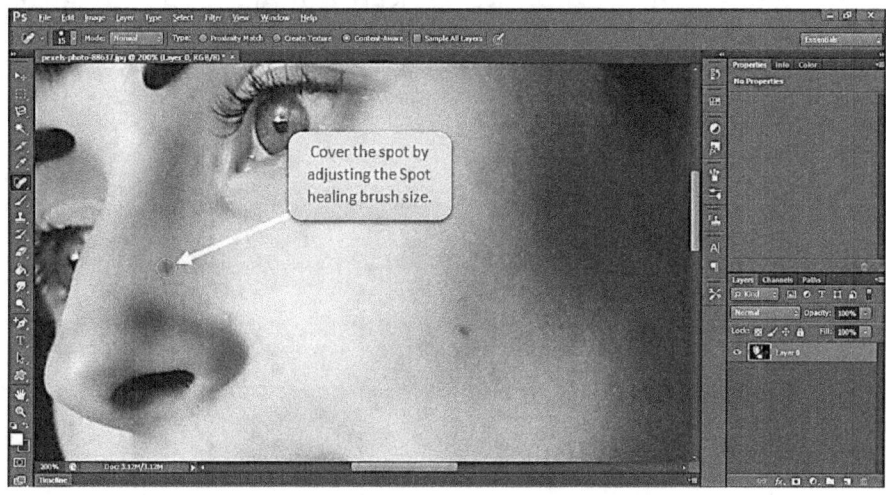

An alternative method involves positioning the cursor over a sample area surrounding the blemish and dragging the cursor across the spot to be removed. During this dragging motion, the tool assimilates the attributes of the sample area, seamlessly applying them to the spot, rendering it consistent with the chosen sample. This drag-and-heal technique streamlines the correction process.

The resulting facial appearance, post-Spot Healing Brush application, demonstrates the tool's efficacy in achieving a seamless integration of the treated area with its surroundings.

Spot Healing Brush tool offers a user-friendly means of effortlessly eliminating imperfections by intelligently borrowing visual attributes from nearby regions. Whether through a simple click or a drag-and-heal maneuver, this tool proves invaluable in achieving a polished and refined output.

The Healing Brush tool

The Healing Brush tool in Photoshop serves to eliminate spots and blemishes from a designated area. By utilizing the color, tone, shading, luminosity, and texture of a chosen sample area, the Healing Brush tool effectively eradicates imperfections. The selection of the sample area can be tailored to specific requirements, even opting for a distant location from the targeted spot area.

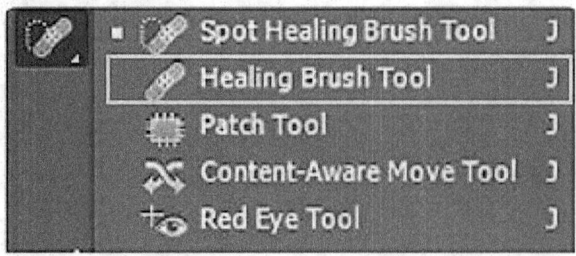

a. Let's open the image using the Photoshop application.

As previously mentioned, the Healing Brush tool addresses spots by incorporating color, shading, luminosity, and texture from a chosen sample area. It's crucial to manually define this sample area.

b. To set the sample area, hold down the Alt key on the keyboard and click on the desired location. While doing this, the cursor will change to.

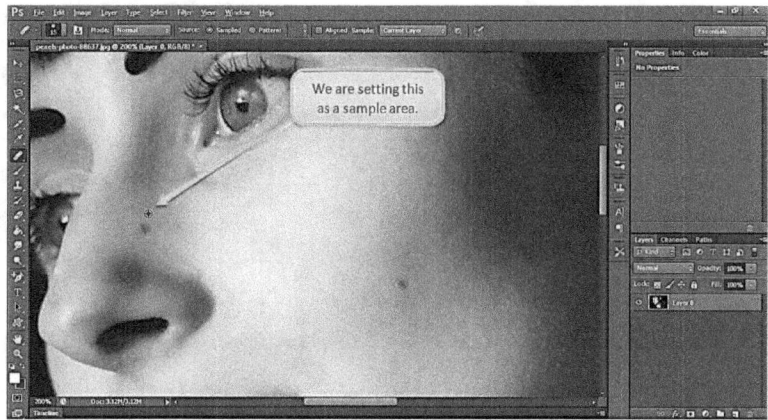

c. Next, drag the cursor over the spot area, and it will apply the sampled color or pattern, as demonstrated below.

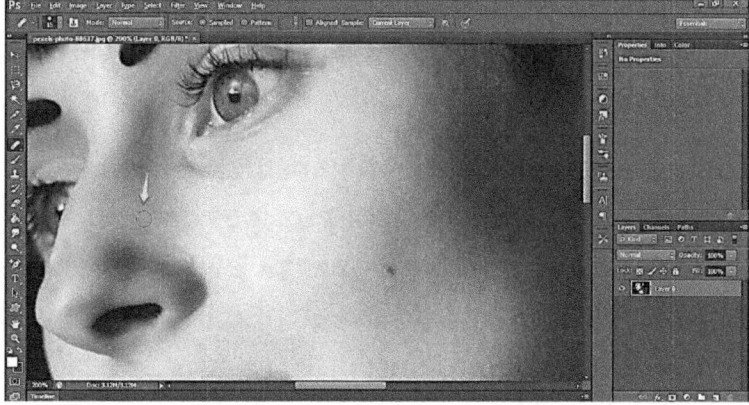

d. Now, let's restore the mole on the nose. To achieve this, set the sample by holding the Alt (Option key on Mac) and clicking on the second mole on the face. Adjust the brush size using the bracket keys on the keyboard.

While dragging the cursor, it's noticeable that the cursor retains the color or pattern from the sampled area (illustrated as a mole in the cursor). Simply click once to reapply it to the nose.

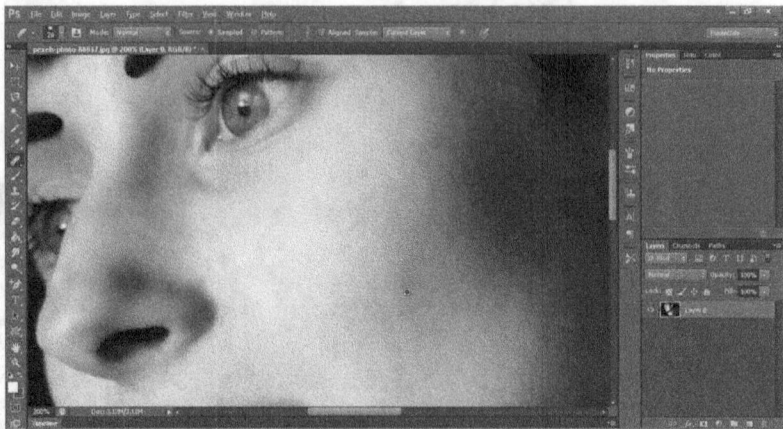

The Photoshop Patch Tool

The Patch tool in Photoshop serves as a versatile instrument for the elimination of imperfections, such as spots, blemishes, or distractions, within an image. Functioning in a manner akin to the healing brush tool, the Patch tool distinguishes itself by allowing users to define a dissymmetric closed path as the sample area selection. This sample area selection is akin to the choices made with the Lasso tool.

While the healing brush tool symmetrically picks patterns and colors in all directions, the Patch tool provides enhanced control over the work area by allowing users to manipulate the selection of the source area. This capability makes the Patch tool particularly well-suited for larger and more dissymmetric images.

To initiate the use of the Patch tool, users first select it from the Photoshop interface. The Patch tool's functionality becomes apparent when making a selection, such as drawing a closed path around a specific element in the image, as demonstrated in the example featuring a bird.

In the Patch tool's option bar, it is crucial to confirm that the appropriate option is enabled.

Case-1, with the Destination option selected, users can move the source object to a destination, essentially cloning the selected object at the chosen destination.

See how we can **clone the bird** in another location using the **Patch tool**.

Case-2, with the Source option enabled, the tool operates in reverse. The selection is moved to a new location, and the background or content of the new source becomes the copied content at the original destination.

The visual representation of these cases showcases the Patch tool's ability to either clone an object to a new location or move the selection to a different area while intelligently preserving the visual continuity of the image.

In both scenarios, the Patch tool proves to be a valuable asset in achieving precise and controlled alterations within an image, allowing for a seamless integration of cloned or relocated elements.

Let's relocate the bird by dragging the mouse cursor to a different position on the canvas. Wherever we release the mouse cursor becomes the source location for the object. In the image below, the new location features a sky background, making it the source location. As the destination should replicate the source, the background from the source is duplicated at the destination.

Below is what the final pic looks like on the **canvas**.

Before Image

After image

USING THE LIQUIFY TOOL

The Liquify tool in Photoshop is a feature that allows users to make flexible and creative adjustments to their images. It provides an intuitive and straightforward means of editing, enabling users to manipulate various aspects of the photo such as shape, size, and distortion. This tool is particularly powerful for creating unique and artistic effects that might be challenging to achieve using other editing tools.

With the Liquify tool, you can easily warp, stretch, or reshape elements within an image, giving you the ability to enhance or exaggerate certain features. This can be useful for retouching portraits, adjusting facial expressions, or even creating surreal and abstract compositions. The real-time preview feature of the Liquify tool allows users to see the changes as they make them, providing immediate feedback and facilitating a more interactive editing process.

Process for using the Liquify tool in Photoshop

To initiate a new Photoshop project and modify an image, start by importing the desired image. Begin by creating a duplicate of the background layer, achieved with "Command + J" or "Ctrl + J."

Following this, right-click on the duplicated layer and convert it into a Smart Object. Why opt for this conversion? It provides flexibility for adjustments using the Liquify tool. If there's a need for fine-tuning or a desire to revert changes later, a Smart Object allows for easy revisions and rollbacks.

Bonus Tip:

For practice with the Liquify tool in Photoshop, consider working on portraits. This tool is commonly employed for retouching people in photos, offering an opportunity to explore the Face Tool, a noteworthy feature in Photoshop.

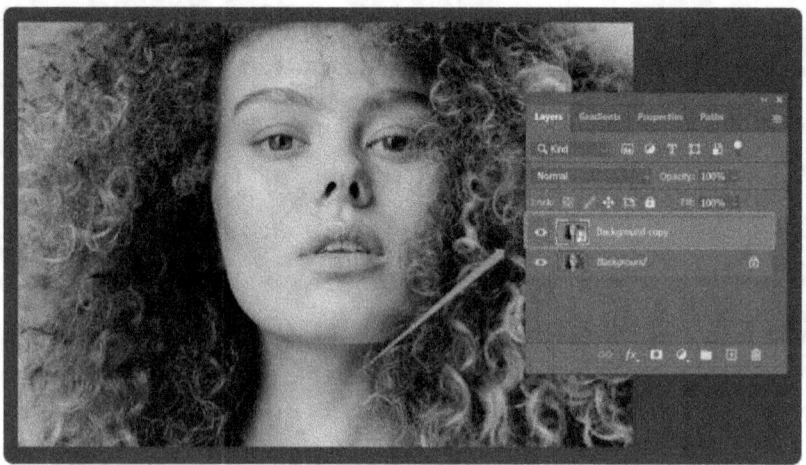

Navigate to the top toolbar and select "Filter." In the dropdown menu, locate Liquify, or swiftly access it by pressing "Shift + Ctrl + X." This action prompts a dialogue box to appear. Despite the abundance of numbers and options, the Liquify tool becomes straightforward once you grasp its essential features within Photoshop.

The Liquify tool workspace is well-organized, with the toolbox conveniently situated on the left-hand side.

Moving on, let's focus on the pressure value, which we can adjust to a lower setting. If you're unfamiliar with using Photoshop's Liquify tool, a pressure value of approximately 20 is a recommended starting point. As you become more accustomed to it, feel free to raise this value according to your preferences.

Effortlessly employing the Forward Warp Tool is a straightforward process. Once you've configured your brush parameters, adjustments can be made wherever necessary.

As demonstrated in the video below, softening the facial lines of the subject is as simple as clicking the left mouse button and gently pushing inward along the edges of the face.

When dealing with photos featuring intricate backgrounds, exercise caution with the Forward Warp Tool to avoid disrupting the horizon line of the background image.

Ensure that your adjustments align with the horizon line rather than roughly dragging the image up or down. Precision is key to maintaining a natural appearance.

In the event that you find yourself going too far, the Reconstruct Tool, positioned below the Forward Warp Tool, functions as an eraser, allowing you to undo changes.

Effectively utilizing the Freeze Mask Tool and Thaw Mask Tool can safeguard areas of the image from distortion.

As depicted in the image below, the Freeze Mask Tool is used to paint over the area you wish to protect. The red area signifies the frozen selection, immune to the effects of the Liquify tool.

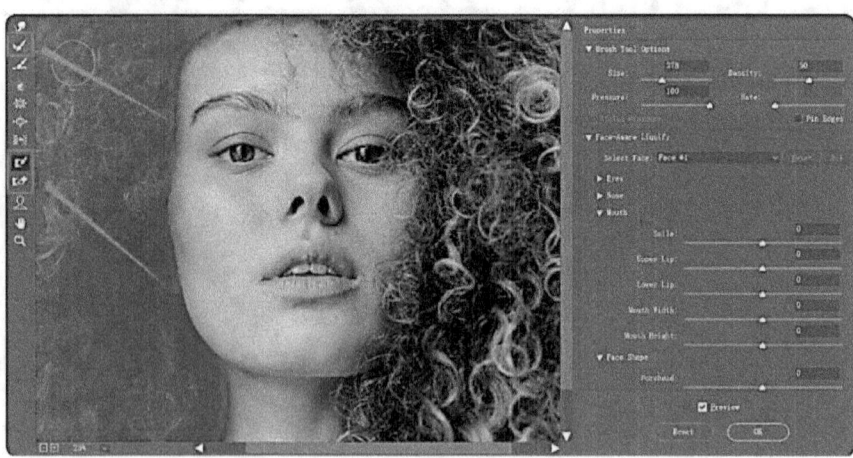

In addition to adjusting the brush tools, the Properties workspace on the right side of Liquify provides further options for refining the image.

In a typical Liquify tool workflow, the usual sequence involves making initial edits using the tools on the left and then fine-tuning with the Properties on the right.

Let's conduct a quick experiment to explore the functionality of the Properties workspace on the right. In a matter of seconds, we can alter the expression of the person in our image to either a smile or a sad look.

Simply focus on the right side of the Liquify tool. In the Face-Aware Liquify section, once the tool recognizes the mouth, you'll find a slider for a smile.

Adjusting the slider to the right or entering a value of 100 allows you to make the person in the image smile.

Moreover, the Properties workspace provides a range of additional features for exploration, including nose height and width, eye size and height, eye distance, face width, and more.

It's akin to the character customization functionality in computer games; you can experiment with various values, shaping the image as if sculpting a face.

While adjusting values may not be as instinctive as manually dragging and reshaping, you can try the Face Tool function located on the left side of the Liquify toolbox. This tool intelligently recognizes different facial elements in the photo. By hovering your cursor over various facial features, Photoshop will astutely identify them, enabling you to manually refine aspects such as the eyes, nose, mouth, and more.

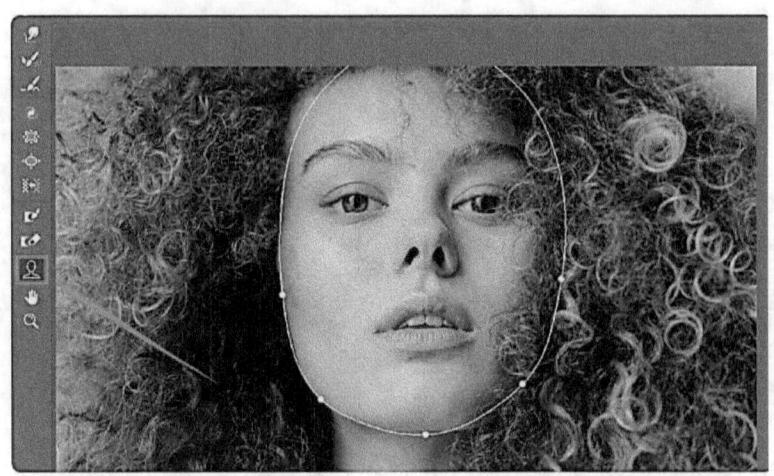

Encountering Challenges with the Liquify Tool in Photoshop

There could be various reasons, such as issues with the color mode or insufficient computer memory. You may find the official answer from Adobe helpful, or you can reach out to Adobe customer service for assistance.

In many instances, the problem may arise from the color mode. Photoshop filters require the RGB color mode. If your project is set to CMYK, navigate to the top menu bar in Photoshop and follow these steps: select Image > Mode > RGB Color. Additionally, adjust to 8 Bits/Channel, and you should be able to use the Liquify tool.

Typically, designers switch to RGB mode to utilize the Liquify tool as needed and then switch back to CMYK mode when they've completed their adjustments.

CHAPTER TEN

TROUBLESHOOTING ISSUES IN PHOTOSHOP

Having Trouble Editing Files from Adobe's Lightroom In Photoshop

Typically, the process is seamless—simply right-clicking on an image and selecting "Edit In > Edit in Adobe Photoshop..." is straightforward, or you can expedite the action using the CTRL+E shortcut.

If Photoshop is running, it will revert to the previous behavior, causing delays, displaying an inability to open, and eventually generating a . TIF file. Therefore, the process will only function if both Photoshop and Photoshop Beta are closed, or if only Photoshop Beta is active.

ADDRESSING GPU AND GRAPHICS DRIVER ISSUES

Update Your Graphics Driver

Updating your graphics driver can resolve various issues, including crashes, incorrectly rendered images and performance issues. Obtain driver updates directly from the video card manufacturer.

- NVIDIA drivers

    To access the NVIDIA Control Panel,

    a. right-click on the desktop. Select "Manage 3D settings."
    b. Click on "Program Settings" and add both Photoshop.exe and sniffer.exe.
    c. Set the Preferred Graphics Processor to the High-performance NVIDIA processor.

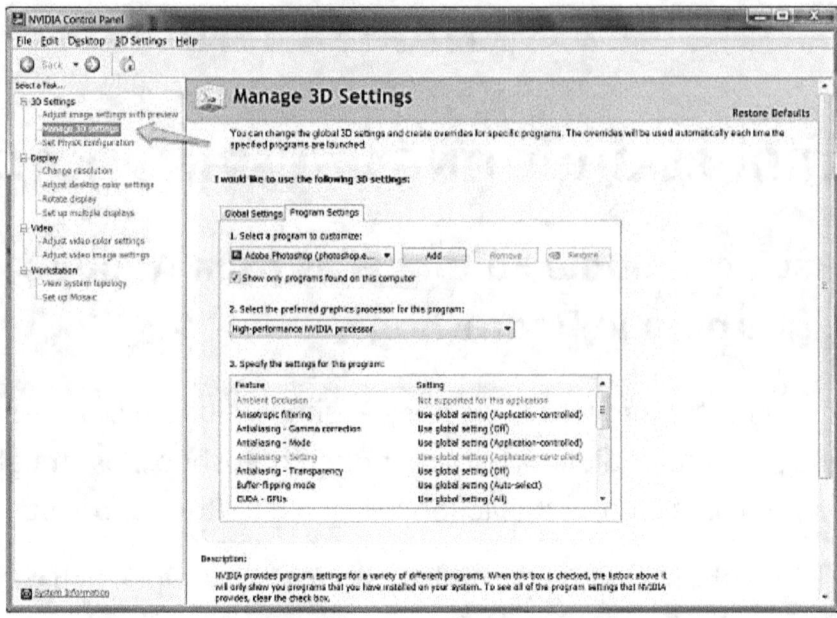

NVIDIA offers a selection of Studio and Game-ready drivers. It is recommended to use Studio drivers.

- AMD drivers

    a. Right-click anywhere on the desktop and choose the AMD Catalyst Control Center or Configure Switchable Graphics.
    b. Click Browse and choose High Performance instead of Power Saving.

- Intel drivers

Most importantly, Ensure you choose the correct driver, as notebook drivers may have a different name than similar desktop drivers. If experiencing flickering or stuttering responsiveness in Photoshop with a GPU that supports G-Sync, disable G-Sync for Photoshop using the NVIDIA control panel. Some video adapter manufacturers may require updates for additional software beyond the video driver; carefully read update instructions and contact the manufacturer if needed.

Check Your Cache Levels Setting

If you've set your Cache Levels to 1 in Photoshop preferences, you may encounter performance issues with graphics processor-dependent features. Reset the Cache Levels to the default setting (4):

1. Choose Edit > Preferences > Performance.

2. Set Cache Levels to 4.

3. Quit and relaunch Photoshop.

4. Retry the steps that caused the problem after relaunching Photoshop.

Reset Your Preferences

Resetting preferences restores Graphics Processor settings to their default state. Refer to "Restore preference files to default" for guidance. After resetting preferences, launch Photoshop and retry the problematic steps.

Enable Older GPU Mode (Pre-2016) Setting

(Optional) For Windows users only:

1. Choose Edit > Preferences > Technology Previews.

2. Enable Older GPU mode (pre-2016).

3. Quit and restart Photoshop for the change to take effect.

This preference forces Photoshop to revert to an alternate rendering engine. While recommended for older GPUs, sometimes newer GPUs may become more stable with this option selected.

Configure Computers with Multiple Graphics Cards

For ultralight laptops and low-end desktops using integrated graphics cards, and higher-end computers with dedicated graphics cards, ensure Photoshop is assigned the High-Performance graphics card for the best experience. If your system has more than one graphics card, confirm that Photoshop is set to use the High-Performance graphics card rather than Integrated Graphics or Power-Saving graphics card for optimal performance. Note that adjusting these settings on laptops may increase battery usage.

Deactivate the Less Powerful Graphics Card

If the previous step fails to address issues with multiple graphics cards, contemplate deactivating one of the graphics cards. Prior to disabling the integrated graphics card, ensure that your monitor's video output is connected to the dedicated graphics card.

To disable a graphics card, navigate to the Device Manager on Windows. Right-click on the card's name in the Device Manager and select the Disable option.

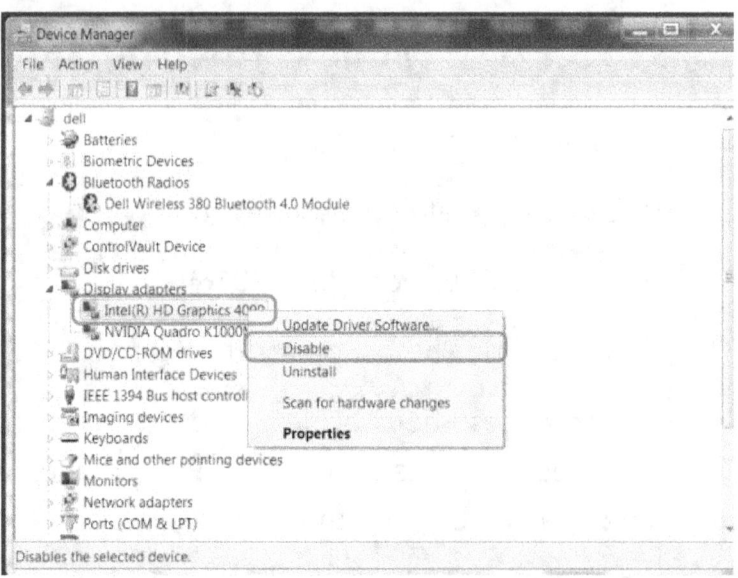

Adjust Your Advanced Settings for Open CL

a. Choose Edit > Preferences > Performance. b. In the Performance panel, click Advanced Settings. c. Disable Open CL. d. Quit and restart Photoshop for the change to take effect.

Note: With the August 2021 (v22.5) release, the Advanced Drawing Mode selector has been removed. For earlier versions, set Drawing Mode to Basic in step c above.

Upon completing the troubleshooting procedures outlined earlier, you can validate the outcomes by activating the "Use Graphics Processor" option within the Preferences > Performance panel. Subsequently, reattempt the steps that initially led to the issue.

macOS

Restart your computer

Some issues may arise immediately after installing or upgrading the Adobe Creative Cloud application and/or Photoshop. After a fresh update or installation of Adobe software, restart your system to check if the symptoms resolve.

Update macOS

Apple integrates GPU drivers into the system software and regularly includes bug fixes in updates. If a system update or security patch is pending, install them and restart your Mac. In cases where your computer cannot install the latest macOS version due to hardware limitations, consider using an older version of Photoshop aligned with your operating system's release date.

- Download macOS installers from other Apple sources

- Keep your Mac up to date

Update Photoshop

Ensure you have the latest version of Photoshop installed, as it incorporates the most recent bug fixes and is designed for optimal stability on systems meeting current macOS and Photoshop requirements.

- As a precaution, keep the last known working version of Photoshop installed alongside the latest version, in case compatibility issues arise. Follow these steps to install multiple versions of Photoshop.

Creative Cloud issues

If you encounter crashes, particularly when opening new files, the Creative Cloud application might be the culprit. Refer to the following documents for assistance with installing or troubleshooting the Creative Cloud desktop app:

- How to install the Creative Cloud desktop application
- How to fix problems with the Creative Cloud desktop application

Turn off the GPU

Check if issues persist by turning off the GPU in Photoshop preferences. Navigate to Photoshop > Preferences > Performance, uncheck "Use Graphics Processor," and then restart Photoshop.

- If problems persist without the GPU, explore additional troubleshooting tips.

- If issues are resolved with the GPU disabled, you may choose to work without it or try the suggestions below.

Re-enable the Use Graphics Processor option

If you disabled the GPU, re-enable it in the Preferences > Performance panel, restart Photoshop, and consider the following suggestions.

Camera Raw issues

If you experience problems specifically when using Adobe Camera Raw, refer to the Camera Raw graphics processor (GPU) FAQ for guidance on crashes, performance issues, or rendering errors.

Turn off Automatic Graphics Switching

For MacBook or MacBook Pro users, disable Automatic Graphics Switching in System Preferences > Energy Saver. Restart Photoshop and observe if the symptoms persist.

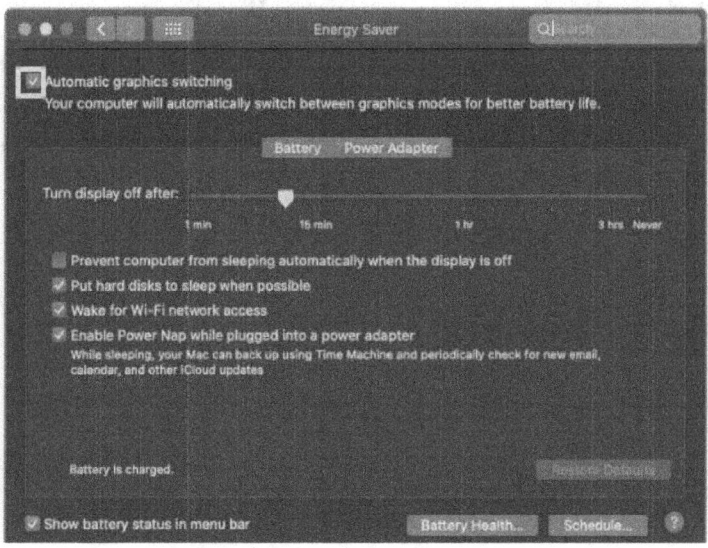

Turn off OpenCL

- Choose Photoshop > Preferences > Performance

- In the Performance panel, click Advanced Settings

- Uncheck 'Use OpenCL'

- Restart Photoshop

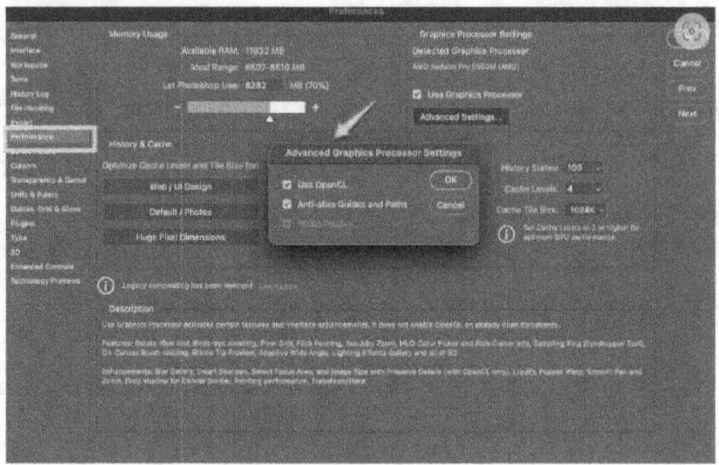

Check your Cache Level setting

If Cache Levels are set to 1 in Photoshop preferences, you may encounter performance issues. Reset the Cache Levels to the default setting (4):

- Choose Photoshop > Preferences > Performance

- Set Cache Levels to 4

- Restart Photoshop

Reset Photoshop preferences

Resetting preferences restores Graphics Processor settings to their default status. Follow the instructions in "Restore preference files to default." After resetting preferences, launch Photoshop and test for errors, as corrupted preference files may be a source of various issues.

ISSUES WITH PHOTOSHOP CRASHES OR FREEZES

To prevent Photoshop crashes, consider closing unnecessary background applications, ensuring your GPU card drivers are up to date, or verifying that your Windows system is updated. If these steps do not resolve the issue, you may attempt clearing the font cache for Photoshop, resetting its settings, or running an SFC scan. A detailed discussion of these solutions is provided below, so please explore further.

Experiencing Photoshop crashes or freezes on your Windows PC? Consider these methods to address the issue:

- Close unnecessary applications.
- Update your graphics drivers.
- Clear the Photoshop font cache.
- Inspect optional and third-party plugins.
- Reset Photoshop preference settings.
- Ensure both Windows and Photoshop are up-to-date.
- Run an SFC scan.

Update Your Graphics Drivers

Graphics drivers play a crucial role in the seamless operation of Adobe Photoshop and other graphics-intensive applications. Outdated or malfunctioning graphics drivers can lead to crashes in Photoshop. If you're facing such issues, it's advisable to update your GPU card drivers to the latest version to potentially resolve the problem.

Follow one of the methods below to update your graphics drivers:

1. Check for Driver Updates via Windows Update to ensure your drivers are up to date.

2. Visit the manufacturer's website to download the latest drivers.

3. Utilize free driver update software for a streamlined update process.

4. If you already have the INF driver file on your computer:

    *   Open Device Manager.

    *   Expand the menu by clicking on "Audio Input and Outputs."

    *   Right-click on your speaker and choose "Update Driver."

    *   Follow the on-screen wizard to complete the update of your audio drivers.

After updating your GPU card drivers, restart your PC and launch Adobe Photoshop. With any luck, the application should no longer experience crashes.

Clear Photoshop Font Cache. A Corrupted font cache can contribute to Photoshop crashes and performance issues. To address this, consider clearing the Photoshop font cache using the following steps:

1. Exit Photoshop and Creative Cloud applications, along with any related tasks.

2. Open File Explorer using the Win+E hotkey and navigate to the following location:

C:\Users\[YourUsername]\AppData\Roaming\Adobe\Adobe Photoshop <version>

3. Add your username and Photoshop version to the above path.

4. Locate the CT Font Cache folder, right-click on it, and choose the "Delete" option to clear the font cache.

5. Ensure to delete it from the Recycle Bin as well.

6. Launch the Photoshop app and check if the problem is resolved.

If Photoshop continues to crash, you may explore additional troubleshooting steps.

Inspect optional and third-party plugins

Random crashes in Photoshop may stem from problematic plugins integrated into the application. If you utilize plugins, it's worth investigating whether they are causing the crashes. Follow these steps:

- Press and hold the Shift button on your keyboard.

- Launch Adobe Photoshop.

- When prompted with the "Skip loading optional and third-party plugins" dialog, choose "Yes."

- Observe if the app still crashes without plugins.

If Photoshop operates smoothly without plugins, it indicates that a specific plugin may be causing the issue. To address this:

- Open File Explorer and navigate to:

C:\Program Files\Adobe\Adobe Photoshop <version>\Plug-ins

- Replace <version> with your Photoshop version.

- Identify potentially problematic plugins and relocate them to another location, such as the Desktop.

- Restart Photoshop and check if the issue is resolved.

Reset Photoshop preference settings

Corrupted Photoshop preference settings could be a potential cause of the problem. To resolve this:

- Create a backup for settings by moving the Adobe Photoshop <version> Settings folder to another location. The path is:

C:\Users\[Your   Username]\AppData\Roaming\Adobe\Adobe Photoshop <version>

- Replace [Your Username] with your username and <version> with the Photoshop version.

- Launch Photoshop, go to Edit > Preferences > General.

- On the Preferences window, select the "Reset Preferences On Quit" option.

- Click OK and relaunch Photoshop to check for resolution.

Ensure Windows and Photoshop are up-to-date

If previous solutions are ineffective, outdated operating system issues might be the culprit. Update Windows to the latest build to resolve compatibility problems and enhance system performance. Install all pending Windows Optional & Driver Updates. Also, update your Photoshop software to the latest version. Afterward, reboot your system and relaunch Photoshop to verify if the crashes persist.

Run an SFC scan System file corruption can lead to application problems.

Execute a System File Checker (SFC) scan to identify and fix corrupted or missing system files. Follow these steps:

- Open Command Prompt as an administrator.

- Enter the command: **SFC /scan now** and wait for the scan to complete.

- Reboot your system after the scan.

- On the next startup, launch Adobe Photoshop to check if the random crashes persist.

If these steps prove ineffective, consider sharing the Photoshop Crash Reports on their forums for further assistance.

SLOW PERFORMANCE OR PHOTOSHOP LAGS

Photoshop Fails to Launch

Surprisingly, encountering difficulties while starting up Photoshop is a prevalent issue. If Photoshop stalls, crashes, or displays a "Loading bottlenecks Halide..." popup, it may indicate damage to your color profiles or system files.

Solution: An effective remedy is to ensure Photoshop is updated to the latest version. If you already have the latest version or are using the Photoshop Trial, consider deleting all files associated with Creative Cloud and Photoshop, then proceed with a reinstallation.

Tool Lag Issues

When using Photoshop on a less powerful PC or laptop, you may experience lag while employing tools like Scrubby Zoom, Animated Zoom, HDR, Filters, Brushes, etc. While some users recommend verifying if your computer meets the minimal requirements, this advice may not be optimal, as Photoshop is optimized to run on less robust systems.

Solution: Confirm that the specific requirements for the functions you intend to use, such as GPU or OpenCL, are met. Adjust the graphics adapter settings accordingly to enhance performance.

Sluggish Performance in Photoshop with Network Drives

When attempting to operate Photoshop with network drives, you may encounter issues such as freezing or unresponsiveness. It's crucial to note that Adobe's technical support only extends to Photoshop and Adobe Bridge when used on your local hard drive.

Solution: Optimize your workflow by copying files from your computer's local drive for photo editing. Edit them in Photoshop locally and then upload the edited files back to the network drive for storage.

Error on Printer/Tablet While Using Photoshop

Sluggish performance or crashes in Photoshop when paired with peripheral devices often stem from improperly configured drivers. Mismatched versions or incompatibility with Photoshop may exist in your printer and tablet drivers.

Adobe developers advise verifying for driver updates or removing the NVIDIA GeForce Experience app. However, if these steps prove ineffective, consider the following solution.

Solution: Unselect "Settings" > "Main" > "Show notifications" or disable Settings > Performance > Advanced settings > Use OpenCL.

Disable Non-Certified Devices

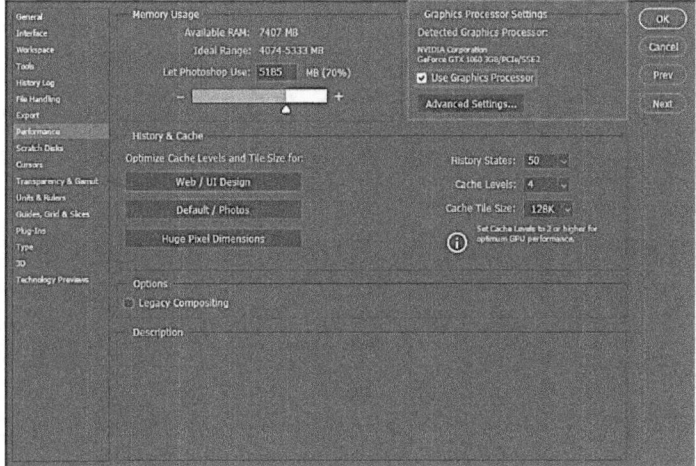

Using Uncertified Equipment in Photoshop is not advisable as it can significantly impede Photoshop's performance in various ways. To ensure that the connected equipment does not compromise your drivers, it is essential to have them updated to the latest version.

If you encounter issues after updating the drivers, consider reverting ***those changes.***

Solution: Disable the graphics processor by navigating to "Settings" > "Performance" and unchecking "Use graphics processor."

Photoshop Utilizes Maximum CPU Power

This issue typically leads to freezing or crashing in Photoshop, often stemming from an underpowered processor or improper configuration.

As a practical solution, removing unnecessary background applications may alleviate the problem. If this proves ineffective, consult the CEPHTMLEngine section for further assistance.

Solution: One of the best, fastest, and simplest solutions is to use the MSConfig utility to optimize your computer as a whole (in automatic mode).

Experiencing Lag in Photoshop with Large Files

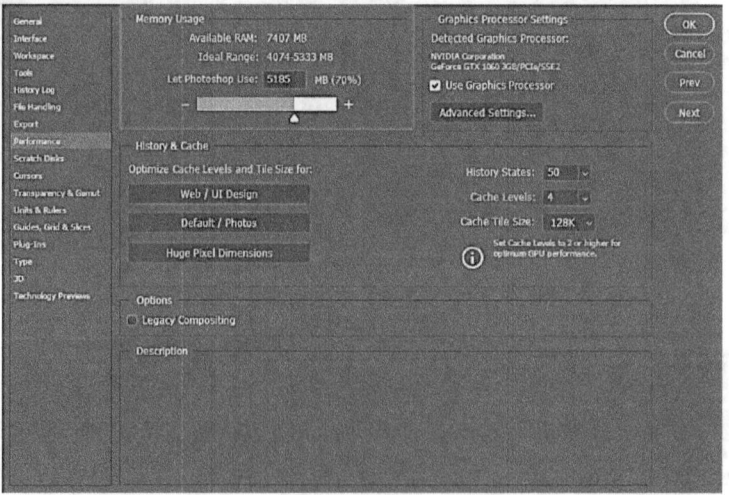

When dealing with large projects or files containing numerous layers on a less powerful PC, you may encounter slow or lagging performance in Photoshop. While some photographers recommend upgrading hardware components such as increasing RAM, it's essential to explore alternative solutions before resorting to hardware enhancements.

Solution: In many cases, addressing the issue of Photoshop running slow can be achieved by allocating sufficient memory. Navigate to "Performance" and increase the allocated memory to a range of 70-85%.

Sluggish File Saving or Project Export

Slow saving or exporting may result from a full hard drive or insufficient administrator rights for saving files in the designated folder. Adobe developers suggest freeing up at least 20% of hard drive space. If this doesn't resolve the issue, consider the following solutions.

Solution: Add scratch discs for use in Photoshop ("Settings" > "Scratch-discs"). Additionally, adjust the virtual system memory/page file size of your operating system.

Photoshop Issues with Monitors

This problem arises when using an older display model. Attempting to update graphics cards or monitor drivers may be a solution, but if unsuccessful, consider the primary solution.

Solution: Switch to a lower-resolution monitor mode in your operating system.

Adjust the Dedicated Cache Size

To accelerate the redrawing of high-resolution documents, Photoshop utilizes image caching. You can set up to eight cache levels and choose from four fragment sizes. Increasing the cache level improves Photoshop's response time, although it may slightly increase image loading times.

There are three cache presets available in the performance settings, each suitable for different Photoshop use cases:

- Web/UI design: Ideal for files with many layers and small or medium pixel sizes, commonly used in web, app, or UI design.

- Default/Photos: Suitable for retouching and editing medium-sized images.

- Huge Pixel Dimensions: Ideal for working with extensive documents, such as panoramic images or 3D graphics.

Modify Graphics Card Settings

Optimizing GPU speed involves keeping video card drivers updated and enabling OpenCL technology, which accelerates the workflow by allowing apps to utilize the graphics processor.

Solution: Turn on OpenCL by accessing "Advanced Graphics Processor Settings" in the "Performance settings" panel and selecting "Use OpenCL."

CHAPTER ELEVEN

SUMMARY

In Adobe Photoshop 2024, an innovative enhancement is introduced to the crop tool with new fill options, notably "generative expand." This feature allows users to expand images beyond their original size, seamlessly filling empty spaces. Particularly beneficial for detailed landscapes and compositing, it enables a versatile and enhanced approach to image manipulation.

Generative Expand emerges as a valuable tool, expanding the horizons of your creative projects. However, prudent and selective application is recommended, recognizing its strengths and limitations in order to extract optimal results and seamlessly integrate expanded elements into your visual narratives.

The Photoshop Dodge and Burn tools boast significant power and versatility. However, their effectiveness can be challenging to harness, particularly if applied with default settings. The guidance provided in this tutorial aims to assist you in attaining favorable outcomes with most photos. It's crucial to note that these tools aren't limited to black and white images; they can yield impressive results when applied to color images as well.

For those seeking an alternative approach, consider utilizing blending modes. A comprehensive tutorial with a video on alternative Dodging and Burning techniques elucidates how to achieve compelling results through this method.

INDEX

www.ingramcontent.com/pod-product-compliance
Lightning Source LLC
Chambersburg PA
CBHW082209290526
45794CB00009B/3485